BLOOD RELATIVE

Portrait of a Mass Murder

Crocker Stephenson

Bonus Books, Inc., Chicago

© **1993 by Bonus Books, Inc.**
All rights reserved

Except for appropriate use in critical reviews or works of scholarship,
the reproduction or use of this work in any form or by any electronic,
mechanical or other means now known or hereafter invented, including photocopying and recording, and in any information storage and
retrieval system is forbidden without the written permission of the
publisher.

97 96 95 94 93   5 4 3 2 1

Library of Congress Catalog Card Number 92-75932

International Standard Book Number: 0-929387-91-0

Bonus Books, Inc.
160 East Illinois Street
Chicago, Illinois 60611

Printed in the United States of America

For the dead remain inside
us, as water
remains inside granite -
hardly at all -
for their job is to
go
away

Robert Bly

The poets themselves, confronted with the murder of their fellow men, proudly declare that their hands are clean. The whole world absentmindedly turns its back on these crimes; the victims have reached the extremity of their disgrace: they are a bore. In ancient times the blood of murder at least produced a religious horror and in this way sanctified the value of life. The real condemnation of the period we live in is, on the contrary, that it leads us to think that it is not blood-thirsty enough. Blood is no longer visible; it does not bespatter the faces of our pharisees visibly enough.

Albert Camus
The Rebel

CONTENTS

FOREWORD

The book you are about to read was constructed out of a vast array of historical residue: newspaper stories, videotapes, photographs, maps, tape recordings, court records, medical examiner's reports, letters, investigative reports, transcripts and the like.

Together, they form the imprint of a small community's brush with horror: the mass murder of five people on July 4, 1987.

While I had fully expected an investigation as long and as intense as the one attached to the Kunz case to have generated an ample supply of such materials, I was quite unprepared for the massive accumulation that awaited me when I began my research in Marathon County more than a year ago.

There were thousands upon thousands of pages of documents contained in court files alone. Virtually an entire shelf in the Marathon County Clerk of Courts' office was given over as a holding place for what was for me a treasure trove of information concerning the murders, the victims, and the suspect, Chris Jacobs III.

And I discovered something more.

Sitting on a file cabinet, well away from the other trial records, was a brown cardboard box—a couple of feet high and several feet long—with Chris Jacobs III's name marked on the lid and the lid tightly taped shut.

I asked for permission to look through the box, but was told it had been sealed by court order shortly following the conclusion of Jacobs' trial. I was allowed to pick it up, though.

It weighed a ton.

In order to gain access to the contents of this box, I was forced to bring suit against the Clerk of Courts, the Sheriff's Department and the District Attorney's Office. Terrence J. Garske, a Wausau attorney who had represented various media interests during the Jacobs trial, agreed to take my case.

Eventually, 286 documents, totaling 1,304 pages, were released to me. Twenty-two documents, totaling 146 pages, remain sealed. They contain the names of minors and of informants and are part of what the Marathon County Sheriff's Department characterizes as 'an ongoing investigation.'

Perhaps it is.

At any rate, the released materials proved to be extremely valuable in completing my book, and I am grateful to my attorney and to Wisconsin's enlightened Open Records law.

While this book is based on these and other sources, I have tried to keep the narrative from being utterly enslaved to them. While most of the dialogues, for example, are based on summary reports, and in several cases on transcripts, some conversations have been altered to reduce (though not remove) redundancies, eliminate confusing characters, or simply to clarify the plot.

This and a variety of other novelistic strategies—detailed descriptions, for example, or moments in which the narrator enters the mind of a character—have been employed not simply to make the story more entertaining, but also to make its events more vivid.

I did not abandon my imagination when attempting to convey a particular place or event, and I encourage readers not to abandon theirs either. I have tried to do more than render the facts of a bizarre set of homicides; I have also tried to evoke their mystery.

I encourage readers to submit to that mystery, to let their imaginations run wild. I believe that is the only way they will get at its truth.

I wish to thank my friend Ed Baumann and my publisher for encouraging me to undertake this project.

I also wish to thank the State Historical Society of Wisconsin for the use of its materials, the staff at the Marathon County Courthouse for their help and for providing me with a place to do my research, and the dozens of reporters whose stories, both print and electronic, served as essential points of reference.

Finally, I would like to thank my wife, Mary Joy O'Meara, and my two children, Jennie and Charlie, for their support, their patience and their sacrifice.

Part I

KENNY

Those farmers in poor circumstances first went crazy because they were ashamed. Then they went even crazier because of the shock of understanding that that intricate webwork of friends, neighbors, officials, purchasing agents, rivals, relatives, creditors and dealers didn't exist to help, sustain and encourage them, didn't even exist to give them a good run for their money, but actually conspired to rob them blind, strip them naked, and steal the pennies off a dead man's eyes.

Michael Lesy
Wisconsin Death Trip

Chapter 1

Queer Antics, Chronic Dementia

From *The Manitowoc Daily Herald*
Dec. 8, 1905:

USED FLATIRON
TO KILL MOTHER

J. Wenzel Kunz, Believed to
Be Insane, Confesses to
Horrible Crime Committed
Last Evening

WOMAN FOUND DEAD, ON BED

Murderer Is Placed Under Arrest
by Police and Tells of Crime on Way
to Jail, Where He is Now Held
for Examination

HAD LONG BEEN
UNBALANCED IN MIND

Family Resided in Kossuth for Years and is Wealthy— Daughter-in-Law Discovers Crime on Return Home From Visit to Neighbors Early in Evening Inquest Called—Kunz in Jail

Using a flatiron as a weapon, J. Wenzel Kunz, believed to be insane, murdered his aged mother, Mrs. Mary Kunz, at the family home, 1121 South Main Street, early last evening, the crime being discovered shortly after its commission, the dead body of the woman gagged, lying across the bed, with blood stains about the floor, on the walls of the room and over the clothing of the aged victim.

Kunz was taken into custody later in the evening and, while being taken to jail by the officers, confessed to the details of the terrible tragedy, the cause of which is unknown.

Discovery of the crime was made by Mrs. Ignatz Kunz, daughter-in-law of the murdered woman, who made her home in the family.

Early in the evening, Mrs. Kunz left the house to visit neighbors, Kunz and his mother, who had been ill, remaining at home alone. The aged woman was resting on the bed when her daughter left home and has evidently been killed without a struggle and no chance to defend herself, the position of the dead body being the same as when Mrs. Kunz had departed.

4

On her return shortly after 6 o'clock, Mrs. Kunz inquired of Kunz as to his mother and received the reply that she was dead. She immediately visited the sleeping chambers to be greeted with the horrifying sight of the aged woman, dead on the bed, a gag in the mouth and eyes open in the ghastly stare of death.

Blood was spattered on the walls and in clots on the floor, and the head of the victim was covered.

Summoning neighbors, Mrs. Kunz dispatched a messenger for an undertaker and to notify authorities, while Kunz remained in the house, apparently taking no interest in the matter. District Attorney Hougen was called and Dr. H. Thurtell viewed the body as a witness at the coroner's inquest which was decided upon. Police Chief Drews, with Officer Menge, arrested Kunz and he was taken to jail for confinement.

While in custody of the officers and enroute to jail, Kunz made a confession, giving details of the murder, which he declared had been accomplished with a flatiron, which was taken from the stove and replaced after the fiendish assault.

The prisoner became hysterical, breaking down completely, but giving no reason for his act.

According to facts as gleaned from the investigation made by the authorities, Mrs. Kunz, who is 70 years of age, had been in feeble health for some time and was cared for by her daughter-in-law, whose husband recently departed for the northern woods to engage in logging operations during the winter.

The murderer, 28 years of age, made his home with his mother and had long exhibited signs of failing mentality, although he had never become violent and the family had no fear of him.

Thursday afternoon, the ironing had been done at the home and the flatirons were still on the stove in the evening. The daughter, with her children, left the house late in the afternoon to make a call at the neighbors and did not return until after 6 o'clock.

The mother had been feeling much impaired in health during the day and Kunz was apparently no different from how he had been previously. After the departure of the daughter, it is supposed that Kunz attacked his mother, though it is not known whether he gagged her before the murder or after. The gag that was used was made from the handkerchief which the aged woman had used during her illness.

Some mystery surrounded the case at the first investigation of the officers and Dr. H. Thurtell, who made the examination of the body, first thought that death might have been due to a hemorrhage and that the handkerchief had been used by the woman herself. The discovery of the wound itself, however, dispelled this theory and with Kunz's confession, the crime was made known.

The flatiron was later found on the stove, covered with blood and matted hair, bearing out the story told by the prisoner. The blow which killed the aged woman was evidently one that had been struck with full force and the scalp had been badly lacerated.

The flatiron was an ordinary, pointed-shaped iron.

Kunz was found by the officers in the house alone with the dead body and offered no resistance to arrest.

He was dressed in several suits of clothes, a heavy overcoat and had his hat on, as though prepared to depart, though he made no effort to escape. Questioned by police, he refused to make a statement until enroute to jail when he confessed.

Ever since the family came to the city, the son has been unemployed, and was of a morose, sullen nature, and while the family believed him to be mentally unbalanced, he had never exhibited a vicious or violent character and there was no fear of him.

Lately Kunz had been imbued with the idea that he desired to marry and had advertised in local German papers and in Chicago and Milwaukee papers. After coming here, Kunz engaged in several enterprises, representing himself as the agent of a mail order house, and at one time advertising to open a store for sale of a patent radiator, but he never made much progress.

Until about two years ago, the Kunz family resided in the town of Kossuth, where Mr. and Mrs. Kunz located in early days and were pioneers. The husband died several years ago, and Mrs. Kunz, and two sons and the family of one, came to the city taking up residence where the crime occurred.

Ignatz, the one son, had been employed in the city and secured work in the northern woods. He was notified of the tragedy and arrived in the city to arrange for the funeral of his mother, which will be held at Kossuth, where the husband and father are buried.

In the inquest, which was held this morning, the jury returned a verdict that Mrs. Kunz came to her death from a blow on the head from a flatiron in the hands of her son, Wenzel Kunz. The jury was composed of Richard Groll, Wenzel Hallads, August Kaems, Albert Neubauer, John Kouthik and Charles Fuerstenburg. District Attorney Hougen was in charge and the evidence of few witnesses was taken, revealing the story as told by Kunz.

Arraigned in municipal court this morning on a charge of murder, Kunz was bound over for examination.

No statement could be secured from the prisoner, who appeared to be in a dazed state, and there is little doubt in the minds of officials that he is insane and an inquiry may be held later to determine the extent of his mental incapacity.

Mrs. Kunz was the mother of five children, all of whom reside in the county, one on the old homestead at King's Bridge. Joseph, one son, is an inmate of the insane asylum, having been committed some years ago.

Wenzel, the son who is charged with the crime, was to have been examined at one time a year ago, but the fact he was not violent and appeared more simple than vicious led to the dropping of the inquiry.

Ignatz has made his home with his mother for some few months, and his wife and children were here while he was at work in the north.

A rumor is current that Mrs. Kunz, the murdered woman, had prepared her will last Saturday, disposing of an estate of considerable value, and it is said that this may have had a bearing on the cause leading to the murder.

Nothing is known of the contents of the document.

From *The Manitowoc Citizen*
Dec. 14, 1905:

On the way to the jail, Chief Drews began to "pump" the murderer and drew from the latter that he had killed his mother with a flatiron.

He stated to the chief that he was worrying over how he was to support his aged mother, as he himself was sickly and could not work. At the jail when searched, Kunz was found to be wearing three pairs of pants and three sets of suspenders, besides his underclothing. Other facts tended to support the supposition that he was mentally unbalanced through sickness.

. . . This morning at nine o'clock, Kunz was arraigned before Judge Schmidt in municipal court, on a warrant sworn out by Dist. Atty. Hougen, charging him with murder of the first degree, conviction of which charge means imprisonment for life in the state's prison at Waupun.

Kunz was represented by Judge Chloupek, and when the case was called, every seat in the small courtroom was crowded to the doors and scores of men and boys were clamoring for admission so they could get a glance at the murderer.

The latter seemed perfectly collected and no more interested than an ordinary spectator. . . .

Many queer antics of Kunz were told by neighbors to substantiate the claim of those that know him that he was mentally imbalanced when he committed the act.

Before the door of the home on South Tenth street was a sign "Kunz Bros.," though Wenzel and his brothers were never in any business. One of the four brothers is now in an insane asylum.

To his counsel it is reported that he intended to commit suicide after he had killed his mother, but did not know how.

From *The Manitowoc Pilot*
Dec. 14, 1905:

. . . The murderer had bound and gagged her before perpetrating the atrocious, cold-blooded crime, that which no more heinous deed has ever been committed in this city. The skull in the back of the head was fractured.

. . . Mrs. Kunz had made a will a few days before her death, and it is thought that this fact may have had some influence in causing the commission of the crime.

It is said that the son was given but a small part of the property, for the reason that he had already received a considerable portion of his share, as his mother had supported him for years.

Testimony in the matter of the inquest of Mrs. Mary Kunz, Mrs. Anna Kunz, sworn:

I live in South Main street together with Mary Kunz. She was my mother-in-law. I was yesterday evening gone about two hours. When I came home, she was dead already. I thought she was sleeping. I didn't take notice. She used to lay in her bed and I thought she was sleeping.

Ed Goetz came over and he looked at her and said she had a hole in her head.

I was so excited, I didn't look at her right away. Afterward, I looked at her.

I had no suspicion who murdered her. Her son was in the house when I left and he came just out of the house when I came back. He didn't say anything to me. I asked him, and he didn't answer.

Testimony in the matter of the inquest of Mrs. Mary Kunz, Dr. Thurtell, sworn:

A young man, Ed Goetz, came to my office yesterday about half past 4 p.m. and asked me to come out to South 10th Street and see a lady who had been found dead and lying across her bed.

I went up there and found the body of an elderly lady lying on the bed with blood stains on her face and hands and a bloody cloth stuffed into her mouth and quite large blood clots and large stains of blood on the bedding.

I at first thought that the death might have been due to hemorrhage of the lungs and that the cloth in her mouth might have been put there by herself in an effort to check the hemorrhage. But when the cloth was removed from her mouth, the part which had been in the mouth was no more stained with blood than the part that projected from the mouth.

Examining her further, I found a large scalp wound at the top of the head, where the scalp was broken and pushed back as if by a dull instrument, leaving a space in the skull about 2½ by 2½ inches completely bare. The skull immediately at the site of the wound was not broken, but was broken further down on the side of the head, enough so that the upper part of the skull could be moved with the finger.

We then began to search for the weapon, and someone in the crowd said that the suspect who had been arrested claimed to have done the deed with a flat iron.

We found three flat irons, two which were free from blood stains and the third had blood stains on one side.

Testimony in the matter of the inquest of Mrs. Mary Kunz, Ed Goetz, sworn:

I live right across the road from the Kunzes. The wife of the brother of the suspect used to come over to our place. That man Wenzel did not come.

Mrs. Annie Kunz came over with her two children and said her mother-in-law was dead. Then my mother went over and looked at the corpse and came right back and told me the place was full of blood.

So I went over there and when I got there I looked at the corpse, then I went for the undertaker.

From *The Manitowoc Daily Herald*
Dec. 14, 1905:

A.P. Schenian, ex-judge of the municipal court, has been retained to defend Wenzel Kunz, who is under arrest, charged with the murder of his mother, and preparations are underway for the trial, which will probably be heard at the January term of the circuit court here.

Kunz is in jail without bonds, and a hearing is to be had in municipal court on the plea of the prisoner. It is generally expected that Kunz will plead insanity and this will raise two issues in the case and may necessitate two trials, one on the insanity plea and, if this is defeated, a second on the murder charge.

From *The Manitowoc Daily Herald*
Jan. 9, 1906:

In connection with the opening of court, J. Wenzel Kunz, who is charged with the murder of his aged mother, was arraigned and refused to utter a word, and appeared the least interested of anyone.

Report of Examining Physicians
Concerning J. Wenzel Kunz
June 18, 1906:

Q: When were the first symptoms of the disease manifested?

A: Always abnormal mentally.

Q: In what way is derangement now manifest?

A: Mental apathy.

Q: Has the patient shown any disposition to injure others?

A: Has murdered his mother.

Q: What relatives have been insane?

A: One brother is now insane. Another brother has been insane. The family is weak-minded.

Q: In your opinion, is the patient insane?

A: Has chronic dementia probably congenital in origin. Will stand in one place for hours without moving. Will hardly answer questions. Appears stupid and takes but little notice of what is taking place around him.

From *The Manitowoc Daily Herald*
June 18, 1906:

Probate court today officially adjudged Wenzel Kunz of unsound mind, and he was committed to the northern hospital at Oshkosh.

The examination was conducted by Drs. Luhmarn, Feazier and Pritchard, and Atty. A. P. Schenian to represent Kunz. Dist. Atty. Hougen consented to forego the prosecution of Kunz on a murder charge because of a belief that the man was and is insane.

Kunz appeared in court with a beard covering his face and presented a most unkempt appearance.

Naturally pale, the beard gave Kunz almost a deathly appearance.

The patient paid little heed to the proceedings, and the examination was conducted largely through the attorney and the papers filed in the case. Kunz, who is 29, killed his mother by a blow from a flatiron.

He had long exhibited signs of failing mentality and there is no question but that he is insane.

It is not expected that his malady is curable.

State of Wisconsin
County Court
Manitowoc County

In the matter of the estate of Mary Kunz, deceased,
21st day of August, 1906:

Frank Kunz, being duly sworn on oath, testified as follows:

Q: What is your name?

A: Frank Kunz.

Q: Where do you live?

A: Town of Kossuth.

Q: You are a son of Mary Kunz, deceased?

A: Yes sir.

Q: She died the 14th of December, 1905?

A: Yes sir.

Q: Where did she die?

A: City of Manitowoc.

Q: When she died, what children did she leave?

A: Frank, Ignatz, John, Joseph, Mary Holman and Wenzel.

Q: Leave any children of a deceased child?

A: Yes. Of Tina Hronek.

Q: Name them.

A: Anna Resba, Fannie Robinson, Frank Hronek, Mary, Rose,
Christina and Bozena.

Q: Do all the heirs live in Manitowoc County?

A: All except Mary Holman. She lives in Chicago.

Q: Where is Joseph now?

A: Manitowoc County Insane Asylum.

Q: And Wenzel?

A: Northern Hospital for the Insane at Winnebago.

Q: What property did your mother leave?

A: A note and a mortgage for $600.

Q: No other property?

A: A little clothes and household furniture. Don't amount to much.

In the matter of the guardianship of Wenzel Kunz, insane, 21st day of August, 1906:

A. P. Schenian, being duly sworn, testified as follows:

> After Wenzel Kunz was arrested, charged with murdering his mother, Mary Kunz, I was retained by his brothers to defend him without expenses to them, the expense to be charged to the estate. During all those times I acted as his attorney and looked up the cases and studied it and collected all the evidence and got it ready for trial in Circuit Court upon the trial for murder. For that, I charge $100, which I think is a very reasonable charge.
> That is about all I have to say in this.

Chapter 2

Waking Up and Going Home

————— 1 —————

Exactly half way between the North Pole and the Equator, and exactly a quarter of the way around the earth from Greenwich, England, is Poniatowski, Wisconsin—the geographic center of the northwestern hemisphere. Here the 90th meridian bisects the 45th parallel in a field of sweet corn a few dozen feet from the edge of a yellow dirt road.

In summer, the field is an industry of insects and vegetation. In winter, it lifts east toward a skyline of emptiness and wind. Only the upper quarter of Holy Family Catholic Church's red brick steeple, and the glittering cross mounted on top, puncture an otherwise immaculate horizon.

Ignatz and Anna Kunz are buried a few miles west of here, in a tiny cemetery just north of the village of Milan. The stone they share faces east, away from the nearby road and toward Bohemia, where Ignatz was born.

They are buried in a land flattened by glaciers, in a confection of crushed granite, limestone and shale. The earth here is encased in a patina of clay, of silt the color of dried yolk. It had been hard work to clear this land. It is still hard work to put a grave in it.

Buried near Ignatz and Anna is a daughter, Ella. Beside her is their only son, Clarence. He shares a slate-gray marker with three sisters—Irene, Marie and Helen—and with a nephew, Randy.

In the center of the cemetery is a primitive statue of Jesus. His hair is painted a flat brown, his lips are bubble gum pink, his eyes are black dots. The wounds on his hands and feet are scarlet.

There is a house across the road. A woman lives there with her husband and three children. She says that whenever she sees someone walking through the cemetery, she turns away from her window.

She says grief is a private thing, as intimate as a kiss.

Sometimes, she'll look out across the road, and someone will have been to the cemetery and they'll have left some flowers behind. Phlox, shasta daisies and aster. Flowers from a kitchen garden, bunched together with a piece of twine and left beside a grave.

Sometimes, the wind will blow the flowers into her yard. It makes her sad.

Once, she picked up some flowers that had blown up to her front door. She placed them in a Mason jar on the kitchen table.

"Where'd the flowers come from?" her husband asked.

Ignatz died in 1952. Anna died in 1965. Ella died in 1975.

Clarence, Irene, Marie, Helen and Randy all died the same night.

July 4, 1987.

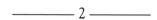

— 2 —

Kenneth J. Kunz was still drunk when he woke up, slumped against the steering wheel of his white Ford Granada. He placed his fingers just below the rim of his seed cap and mashed the palms of his hands into his eyes. He drew his hands down the front of his face and wiped his nose with the back of his left hand.

There was an unfinished can of Pabst Blue Ribbon beer propped on the dashboard.

Kenny killed it.

Ever since he was arrested for drunken driving a few years back, and lost his license, and had to rely on Ken Fasse to drive him everywhere, Kenny tried not to drive when he was feeling really smashed.

"Don't want to tangle with no bubble-top," he'd say.

Sometimes Kenny would just pull off the road, roll down the window a crack, and fall asleep. A truck might speed by and shake his car, and Kenny would open his eyes. He wouldn't move his head, just stare up through the windshield at the reeling stars. Then he'd go back to sleep. If the stars didn't reel, he'd climb out of his car and take a piss. Then he'd drive home.

Just as often, Kenny would sleep at the Kraft Inc. cheese plant in Milan, where he had worked for more than 30 years. It was a convenient, though somewhat risky, place to sleep off a drunk. A few months earlier, the plant manager, Eileen Moore, found out Kenny had been tucking beers into his lunch box and sleeping at the plant at night.

It wasn't the first time Kenny had been caught drinking on the job, and Moore had to tell him to stop coming into the building after working hours. She had to tell him that he would be fired if he was ever caught drinking at work again.

Eileen Moore didn't enjoy reprimanding Kenny. It made her feel like a bully. He was so shy, she thought. So timid. Why he blushed just about anytime she said, "Hi." The blush would start just above his eyebrows and drop down his face like a curtain, leaving the top of his head white as curd. And those big, goofy ears of his. Good God. They'd turn crimson. He was just about deaf, she found out back in 1985, when everyone in the plant was given a hearing test.

Until the test, she thought Kenny was some kind of, you know, some kind of idiot. Or something.

Sweet, though.

It's just that she always had to tell him things twice. And he hardly ever said a word. When he did, it was usually just a whisper.

He would turn his head away from her, just about placing his chin against his far shoulder, and he'd whisper, and his voice was so sere and soft. Like the voice of a very old man. Like he was talking in his sleep.

Perhaps it was the hearing problem, she wasn't sure, but it was almost as if Kenny inhabited himself, living just below the surface of his own skin. In all the years she had known him, she had hardly ever seen his face change expression. Always the same droopy sadness.

It seemed as if the only emotion he was capable of expressing with any depth at all was shame.

He was a pretty good worker, though. He ran the pasteurizer. Sometimes he smelled pretty bad, and once in a while she had to tell him to change his clothes.

He was like a child, really.

Sweet.

The nice thing about the cheese plant was its location: right beside Wally and Bernie's tavern.

"Wally's" is what everybody called it, though Wally was dead. Bernie, his wife, ran the place. Not a whole lot to Wally's: a jukebox, a pool table, a bar, a cement floor, a dog named Freddie. Freddie was a poodle. He belonged to Bernie. No cigarette machine. Bernie sold cigarettes right out of a couple of cartons she kept stashed behind the bar. The jukebox had some Charlie Pride and some Dwight Yoakam. It had Don Peachy's "Good Morning Polka," and a couple of tunes by the Polka Stars.

The most striking things about the bar were its trophies. Dozens and dozens of them. Most were earned in drinking matches that followed softball games with other taps. The tallest was made from 15 Pabst Blue Ribbon cans. It was five tiers tall, and had a batter perched on top. The trophy said:

"FIRST PLACE."

"Not fancy, but the beer's cold and Bernie there's tolerant," a drunk old man said. Three other men stood nearby. There were no women at Wally's. Except Bernie. Freddie came close. One of the men was uttering obscenities, just to make his buddies laugh.

"Cunt," he said.

"Pecker."

"Shit for brains."

The drunk old man held his beer in his left hand. His right arm was missing. He said it had been torn off by a corn picker.

Kenny slipped the emptied Pabst can into a paper bag and noticed a red streak across the hand he had used to wipe his nose. He licked his upper lip and tasted blood. He flipped on the car's interior light and studied his nose in the rear-view mirror. Drops of blood formed on the end of it and dripped onto his vinyl blue jacket.

"Shit," he said.

He dug through the change in his pants pockets and found a couple of wads of tissue and pressed them under his nose. He laid his head back and waited for the bleeding to stop.

"Shit," he said.

A few minutes, and the bleeding stopped. Kenny tucked the bloodied tissues into the bag with the beer cans. He started his car and headed home.

It had been the Fourth of July. The start of a week's vacation. In the back seat of his car, Kenny had stashed a grocery bag filled with Roman Candles, fire crackers, cherry bombs and rockets. Kenny had planned to celebrate.

But he had spent the night in the truck bay of the cheese plant, going through a 24-pack of Pabst he had purchased at Wally's.

Kenny was able not to think about it.

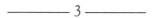

—————— 3 ——————

The Kunzes' 108-acre farm, six miles west of the little village of Athens, belonged to Kenny's uncle, Clarence, who bought the land in 1949 for about $2,000.

Clarence built the house himself. Ignatz helped to lay the foundation, and Kenny, who was 16 at the time, sawed a few boards, pounded a few nails, but mostly it was Clarence's house. Everyone in the family called it that—Clarence's House. It had four rooms, all on the first floor, a basement and an attic.

The house was unheated and had no pump, no running water. There was an outhouse in a thicket of trees ten feet or so from the back of the house. Cooking was accomplished on a big green enameled wood stove attached to a cider block chimney in the kitchen.

For decades, everybody lived in Clarence's house, except Germaine, Kenny's aunt, the only one of Ignatz and Anna's children to marry. Then, in the early 1980s, Kenny decided he needed a place of his own. He put together a few dollars and bought a tiny trailer—a rusty camper, really—and moved out.

Kenny's move toward independence didn't take him very far. He parked the trailer beside a stack of firewood about 100 feet from Clarence's front door.

That left the three sisters—Irene, Marie and Helen—and Helen's son, Randy, all living with Clarence in the house.

It made for tight quarters.

The back room that had belonged to Kenny had always been terribly cold—even during the summer it seemed drafty—and after Kenny moved out, the Kunzes let it fill with boxes, a couple of broken wood stoves and a wrecked couch. After a few years, they closed it off entirely.

Helen and Randy shared a bed in the other back room. Its gypsum board walls were patched with duct tape and painted with a thin coat of deep blue. The walls were decorated with seven or eight calendars and a beer poster. The room contained two television sets. One, a color TV, was hooked to a VCR Kenny had bought for Christmas a few years back.

At the foot of the bed were piles of boxes and a big stuffed chair, which was placed with its back to a doorway that opened into the kitchen.

Three things took up most of the space in the kitchen: the Moderne Green Windsor Montgomery Ward & Co. wood stove, a casket-sized Coronado Super freezer, and a sweaty refrigerator. There were also three small tables stuffed in there, and a couple of chairs, too. One doorway opened to the living room, and another opened to an enclosed porch. When the front door opened, it pushed aside a coil of red fly-paper that hung from the ceiling.

Shut the door, and the strip swung back and forth.

The only picture on the wall was a calendar, this one from the Athens Cooperative. In July 1987, it showed a herd of Herefords grazing in a field of grass the color of lime Jello.

The feature recipe for the month was Tuna Vegetable Pilaf.

Helen, who did all the cooking, bought most of the food, and she needed both the big white freezer and the refrigerator to hold everything.

Every other Thursday, someone from Pinter Packing Co. would stop by and sell Helen meat. Sausages. Steaks. Lamb chops. Veal. Occasionally, she bought everything on the truck, sometimes spending as much as $125 at a time. She always paid in cash, stripping $10 and $20 and even $100 bills from an inch-thick wad of money she pulled from her purse.

Sometimes, if Kenny was around, he'd buy half a ham. Always paid cash.

The Kunzes were good customers, but the Pinter delivery men hated to stop at their house. It was dark and smelled awful and there were cats everywhere and packs of dogs running around inside and howling away outside and specter-thin old people dressed in turn-of-the century clothing peering out from the shadows of door jambs and from behind pieces of busted furniture.

Brian Pinter made them go anyway, though he didn't particularly enjoy going there himself. Frankly, it gave him the creeps. One time, he said, he was hauling a few bags of groceries in for Helen, and there, on the stove, was a dead cat.

Well, it looked dead, anyway. That's what he told everyone.

He'd never forget that, he said.

Clarence, Irene and Marie shared the living room.

23

Clarence slept on a narrow bed pushed against the north wall, beneath a small and curtainless window. The room was heated by a huge wood stove from the Laclede-Oak Carbon Stove and Range Co., and in front of the stove were Irene and Marie's beds.

That left little room for anything else, and what with the table, half a dozen chairs, the wood cabinets, the metal file cabinet, the shelves, the TV, the telephone, the stack of wood and the boxes upon boxes, the tiny yellow room, with its white linoleum floor, was a cramped nest that reeked of fuel oil, animal feces, and cuspidors of expectorated Summer-Time Long Cut Tobacco.

Clarence's house was never a palace, but for several decades, Clarence farmed, maintained about 15 or so head of of dairy cattle and even made a little money. Then he developed a heart ailment, everyone else started getting old, the barn collapsed in a windstorm one night, no one felt quite up to fixing it and the place pretty much went to hell.

Town Assessor Betty Auner figured the farm was worth $29,550. That included the house, which she assessed at $300.

"It wasn't many years ago that if Clarence took off his pants, they'd stand up by themselves," a neighbor said. "He worked so hard, he was always covered with grime."

But now, at 76, Clarence hardly bothered to put his pants on at all. He stood just 5 feet 6 inches and weighed no more than 120 pounds. He walked with a cane, and he had grown so feeble that it took him forever just to walk up to the road and gather the mail.

The dogs would run before him, reach the mailbox, and run back. Back and forth. Back and forth. Howling.

Leonard Seidler, who had worked at the feed mill in Milan for 28 years, said that even after the Kunzes got rid of their dairy cows, they had so many dogs that they still had to come to the mill for feed.

Clarence would drive his three sisters into Milan and while Helen bought feed, he would visit a tavern across the street. Irene and

Marie would wait in the car. After a while, Helen would pull Clarence out of the bar, and he would drive them home.

In the last few years, though, Clarence almost never left the farm.

He had been hospitalized three times, and after each stay, Germaine would take him to live with her in her tidy little house in Abbotsford. She made sure he took baths, and she dressed him in flannel pajamas and a nice plaid robe.

She brought him coffee. Cooked him hot meals. Put pillows behind his head. But he was always anxious to get home.

There, weeks might pass before he'd bother to shave. He just about never bathed. His toe nails would grow so thick and long that they'd start to curl and crack and yellow.

It hurt to walk, so he pretty much just stayed in bed.

The last time Kenny would see his uncle alive, just after dinner on July 4th, Clarence was already asleep, his bald head, his unshaven face, propped upon a dirty pillow, his body a narrow presence beneath a thin blue blanket.

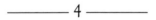

—————— 4 ——————

From a pamphlet published by a land speculator urging settlers, seeking farm land, to locate in northern Wisconsin:

> "If you want land where trout streams murmur and broad rivers gleam through walls of cedar, and the gold of buttercups is mingled with the white bloom of clover, then I have seen the fair land of which you dream, a country gentle, undulating, like the billows of the sea, fruitful and rich in all the grasses that a shepherd loves."

It had been Anna's idea to leave Manitowoc after her mother-in-law's murder.

Anna had a sister near Athens whose husband needed someone to do some masonry work. Ignatz saw a chance to make a new start. So in 1914, Ignatz bought a 40-acre farm from the Rietbrock Land & Lumber Company.

Frederick Rietbrock was a wealthy former Milwaukee County District Attorney and one of the great lumber lords of the Wisconsin Cutover.

While Rietbrock's land company extolled the healthy virtues and natural wonders of simple north woods living, Rietbrock himself—as well many of his fellow millionaire industrialists and lumber barons—preferred to live in Milwaukee.

But he allowed himself frequent visits to Marathon County, whenever business required him to do so, though, once he got back to the city, he would say these trips were just all too brief.

During one particularly cold week of the winter logging season, lumber camp thermometers failed to climb above 20 below zero. Rietbrock's frost-bitten loggers complained that it was too damn cold to work.

Rietbrock appeared in the camp within the day. He wore a black beaver-skin hat and black beaver-skin boots. His thick white beard hung down over his black double-breasted beaver-skin coat.

He said very little. He simply ripped a branch down from a tree and broke every thermometer in camp.

The work stoppage was over.

Rietbrock's company showed an equal measure of compassion as, toward the end of the lumbering boom, it began to unload its vast holdings of land. Patently unsuitable for farming, and shorn of the timber that constituted its only real value, the land had become worthless, nothing more that a tax liability.

So the company, and many like it, began marketing the land to immigrants and the urban poor—people whose ignorance of farming, or whose desire for self-sufficiency, made them easy prey.

Once the land was sold, the lumber companies pulled out, leaving behind a region incapable of generating the economy needed to support the scores upon scores of families that had been lured there.

And so the Wisconsin Cutover collapsed into a poverty that was as extreme and as debilitating as that of the southern Appalachians.

From *The New York Times*
June 3, 1934:

WILDERNESS SLUMS
WORRY WISCONSIN

2,000 Families Without Means of Livelihood Live in Squalor on Cutover Lands

Lost in the cutover land of northern Wisconsin, where farming has failed and the natural forest crop has been forgotten too long, 2,000 stranded families are living in homes that are literally wilderness slums.

Sod houses, crumbling shacks and old log cabins are the dwellings of these children of the men who came north to work in the temporary hemlock and pulpwood industries, or to farm the newly cleared land in a region where winter is severe and nine months long.

The situation is the cause of considerable worry on the part of State authorities because these wilderness slum dwellers have no opportunity to earn money and their land will not grow food.

They are practically out of touch with civilization.

They live in physical and often moral squalor and are so scattered and isolated in the woods that they do not possess a mass consciousness of their situation.

This is not the "backwoods" life of the Wisconsin pioneers who had energy and were surrounded by the wealth of giant white pine trees, but the depressed state of a people with no future living on a land stripped of its natural resources.

Eighty years ago white pine lumbering reached industrial importance in Wisconsin, and for a decade after 1892 this State led in lumber production. Millions of feet of logs were floated from the north to the original sawmill towns which had been established at falls in rivers in the Wisconsin, Fox, Kickapoo and Mississippi valleys. Farming grew about the towns to supply local needs. Money came to the men in the white pine harvest, railroads were built, various industries were encouraged and farming and dairy work were developed. . . .

When the new century came there was little pine left—the rush was over. But this cutting had been a destructive selective attack on the forests, so promoters started the hardwood-hemlock industry and began the pulpwood harvest.

Subsidized northern farm colonization was begun by the State, land companies were encouraged and marshes were drained to provide more and more farm land in northern Wisconsin. Thousands of acres of natural cover for land and water animals were destroyed to make farms.

But times had changed, and the future had been read poorly.

The new lumber boon passed and the farms would not grow crops. Hardwood logs could not be floated down the streams and rail transportation was too costly, so portable sawmills were taken into the woods and the life of the towns was short.

These abandoned towns of the second lumber era may be seen in all northern Wisconsin counties. Stores are boarded up and the hotel door swings open to hitchhikers who seek free shelter. Sometimes a family or two, unable to leave when the last mill closed, linger. . . .

As matters stand, the 2,000 families in the back country live almost wholly on State, county and federal aid.

Impoverished, wrongly situated and left behind by
lumber companies, these people seem to have suffered
with the denuded land.

Ignatz's piece of denuded land—which was just west of the
farm Clarence would someday own—came with an 18-foot-by-20-foot
log home.

It had two rooms: one upstairs, where everybody slept, and one
downstairs, where there was a big wood stove. At Christmas, a
relative in Chicago would send the Kunzes a bushel of oranges. Ignatz
played the concertina and sang in a sweet tenor voice.

The farm had a lean-to style barn and no outhouse. A neighbor,
Helen Bergmann, said she remembered that the family conducted
their toilet behind a pile of rocks. She said heads would peek over the
rocks whenever someone happened by.

A one-room schoolhouse was located less than a mile north, and
the Kunzes sent their children there. Germaine and Irene went all the
way through the 8th grade. Ella, not quite that far.

Marie, who was retarded, went for a few years, but never learned
to write, not even her name. Schoolmates described her as hunched
back, tall and incredibly thin. She never talked, but they said, just
made noises and gestured with her hands.

By the time of her murder, she had grown so obscure that
people who had known the family for years were not aware that she
even existed.

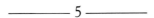

— 5 —

Helen became pregnant with Kenny in April 1932, about a
month after her 15th birthday. She was in the 7th grade, and the
birth occurred over Christmas vacation.

Helen never missed a day of school that year. Her teacher had
promised to give $1 to each child who had perfect attendance.

When Ignatz and Anna discovered Helen's pregnancy, they summoned the police to their home. Helen told them she had been sexually assaulted by Frank Gumz, a 40-year-old bootlegger who lived across the road.

From a transcript of testimony given on July 7, 1933, in the case of State of Wisconsin vs. Frank Gumz:

By District Attorney O.L. Ringle:

Q: Where do you live, Helen? What town do you live in?

A: Johnson.

Q: Does your father live there with you?

A: Yes.

Q: Do you know Mr. Gumz?

A: Yes.

Q: Where does he live?

A: Town of Johnson.

Q: Where does he live with reference to your house? That is, how far away from your house does he live?

A: Not very far.

Q: Does Mr. Gumz live right across the road from you?

A: Yes.

Q: How old are you now?

A: 16.

Q: How old were you on the first of April, a year ago?

A: 15.

Q: What is the date of your birthday?

A: March 27.

Q: Did Mr. Gumz do anything to you about in April, a year ago?

A: Yes.

Q: What did he do?

(no reply)

Q: Do you understand what is meant by sexual intercourse?

A: Yes.

Q: Do you know what that is?

A: Yes.

Q: That is when a man takes his private parts and puts it into a girl's parts. You understand that?

A: Yes.

Q: Will you tell the judge whether Mr. Gumz had sexual intercourse with you April 1932—that is, a year ago. Did he, or did he not?

A: Yes.

Q: Where did that take place? Or where did he do that?

A: By his place.

Q: You mean by his farm?

A: Yes.

Q: At what place on the farm?

A: In the barn.

Q: What were you doing over at Mr. Gumz's place at that time?

A: Playing.

Q: Playing with whom?

A: With his girl.

Q: What is that girl's name?

A: Violet.

Q: How old is Violet?

A: 11.

Q: Just what did Mr. Gumz do to you while you were playing? Where did he take you?

A: In the barn.

Q: After you got into the barn, what did he do? Or where did he take you?

A: In the hay mow.

Q: How did he get up in the hay mow?

A: With a ladder.

Q: Did you go up there alone, or did he take you up with him?

A: No.

Q: What is that?

A: No.

Q: How?

A: He took me with him.

Q: You mean by that, that he carried you up there?

A: Yes.

Q: Was it after he got you up in the hay mow that he did this thing to you?

A: Yes.

Q: That was when he did it, was it?

A: Yes.

Q: Was that the only time he ever did that to you?

A: Yes.

Q: Just once?

A: Yes.

Q: Or did he do it again after that?

A: No.

Ringle: Of course, she is a very unwilling and very unusual witness. I think on her preliminary she testified he did that again after that.

Judge A.H. Reid: Yes, she so testified, according to the record.

Q: Do you remember you were in court once before?

A: Yes.

Q: Do you remember you said at that time that he did it again about a week after that?

A: Yes.

Q: Do you remember that?

A: Yes.

Q: Now, what do you want us to understand—that he did it again, or did it just that once?

A: Yes.

Q: What is that?

A: Yes.

Q: What do you mean by that?

A: Did it once.

Q: Just that once?

A: Yes.

Q: He did it just once?

A: Yes.

Q: Is that right?

A: Yes.

Q: Did you have a baby?

A: Yes.

Q: How long ago?

A: About six months.

Q: Do you remember the date when that baby was born?

A: December 23.

Q: That is December 23—last December, you mean.

A: Yes.

Q: What was that baby—a boy or a girl?

A: Boy.

Q: And the baby is living now?

A: Yes.

Q: Where were you when the baby was born?

A: In the house.

Q: At your father's house?

A: Yes.

Q: When Mr. Gumz carried you up the ladder into the hay mow there, did he say anything?

A: I shouldn't say anything.

Q: Told you not to say anything?

A: Yes.

Q: What time of day was this?

A: Evening.

Q: Was it after supper or before supper?

A: After supper.

Q: And do you know about what time it was after supper?

A: About eight.

Q: Was it dark then?

A: Yes.

Q: Where had Mr. Gumz been while you were playing with his daughter? What was he doing?

(No reply)

Q: Was he working there?

(No reply)

Q: Do you know what he had been doing?

A: No.

Ringle: I guess that's all.

By Judge A.H. Reid:

Q: Was there anybody in the barn but you and Mr. Gumz at the time?

A: Yes.

Q: Who was there besides you and Mr. Gumz?

(No reply)

Q: Was there anyone?

A: No.

Q: Where was the girl—where was Lillian?

(No reply)

Q: Did she go in the barn?

A: No.

Q: Where was she?

A: House.

Q: Where were you when Mr. Gumz asked you to go into the barn?

A: By the house.

Q: Was that far from the barn?

A: No.

Q: How far? As far as the width of this room?

A: Yes.

Q: Any further?

A: No.

Cross examination by Allan Park:

Q: Helen, do you know what date this act occurred? Do you what date it was that Mr. Gumz took you up in the barn that time?

A: No.

Q: You remember you were before the court last August?

A: No.

Q: You remember testifying in court about a year ago, don't you, Helen?

A: Yes.

Q: And do you remember at the time telling the court that this act occurred on the first day of April?

A: Yes.

Q: It was dark at that time, wasn't it?

A: Yes.

Q: Where there any lights out in the yard that shown out in the yard by which you could play, or any lights shining out from the kitchen or the barn that you could play by?

A: No.

Q: Has Mr. Gumz any other children besides Violet?

A: Yes.

Q: How many?

(No reply)

Q: Seven?

A: Yes.

Q: And where were these children at the time you and Violet were playing out in the yard?

A: I don't know.

Q: You didn't see them around yourself, so you don't know where they were, is that right?

A: No.

Q: Do you know where Mrs. Gumz was?

A: No.

Q: Did you see her that evening at all?

A: No.

Q: Did you make any noise when he took you into the barn?

A: Yes.

Q: What did you do?

A: Tried to get away.

Q: Did you cry out, or shout, or scream, or do anything of that sort?

A: No.

Q: You just tried to get away?

A: Yes.

Q: Did you speak at all? Did you speak out loud at all when he was taking you into the barn?

A: No.

Q: Did you know what he was taking you there for?

A: No.

Q: Didn't you have any idea?

A: No.

Q: How did you learn what sexual intercourse means? How did you know that? Who told you about it?

(No reply)

Q: Do you remember who told you first what that means?

A: No.

Q: You don't remember that. Did you tell your mother anything about this?

A: No.

Q: When did you first talk about this to anyone?

A: In May.

Q: Who did you tell then?

A: Oldest girl.

Q: What oldest girl? You mean your sister?

A: Yes.

Q: That was in May. That was a month or two after this happened, was it?

A: Yes.

Allan Park wanted to raise the possibility that Helen might have been impregnated by her brother, Clarence, and he called Gumz's son, also named Clarence, to testify in his father's behalf. Clarence Gumz testified that he often saw Helen and her brother go into the barn together. Clarence Gumz said that when he went to play Parcheesi or cards with the Kunz children "sometimes (Helen and Clarence) were in the barn, and then most of the time we had to wait a little while."

Q: The rest of the Kunz family would be in the house?

A: Yes.

Q: And you would be waiting for those two to come out of the barn?

A: Yes.

O.L. Ringle called Anna Kunz to rebut the implications raised by Clarence Gumz's testimony:

Q: This house that you live in—what sort of house is that? How large a house is that?

A: The house is 18 by 20.

Q: How many rooms are there downstairs?

A: Only one room. And one room upstairs.

Q: Where does your family sleep?

A: We sleep all upstairs, and Helen sleeps downstairs.

Q: All of you sleep upstairs?

A: Yes, we all sleep upstairs.

Q: Where did you all sleep, say, a year ago last April—a year ago last April?

A: Upstairs.

Q: You all slept upstairs. Did Helen sleep upstairs, too?

A: Yes, she slept upstairs, too.

Q: This boy Clarence. Is that his name?

A: Yes.

Q: How old is he?

A: 22.

Q: Helen is how old?

A: 16.

Q: Have you ever noticed anything wrong about the relationship between Helen and your boy?

A: No. I didn't know nothing wrong.

Q: Did you ever see anything?

A: No, I never see anything.

Q: You heard this statement here? That your son and Helen very frequently would go into the barn together?

A: To the barn? No. They never went to the barn. Sometimes the boy went to the barn. Can't a boy and girl go to the barn milking?

Q: What did they do there?

A: They didn't do nothing there.

Q: Were they there to do any work?

A: They didn't go together in the barn.

Q: Did they have any work to do?

A: They always got some work to do.

Q: So that if they went in the barn, did they do any milking. Did they milk cows?

A: Helen don't milk cows.

Q: Who does?

A: Clarence and the oldest girl milks cows. And sometimes I milk cows too—when he's busy.

Q: Did you ever see Clarence and Helen in the barn together—

A: No, I never seen—

Q: Doing anything wrong?

A: No, I never seen anything wrong.

Ringle: That is all.

Park: No cross examination.

Gumz had witnesses to testify that he was elsewhere at the time of the assault. He got up on the stand himself and swore he had been out looking for a horse. His wife, Amanda, testified that he had not been home during most of the day. She testified that she remembered the day "just like it was like today" because "it was raining in the morning something terrible."

Judge A.H. Reid said, "If this little girl was brought up a different way—had a different mentality and different characteristics, I would have thought it was impossible that this could have happened without her making an outcry or without immediately going to her mother."

Reid said, "The absence of those things are rather important facts."

But, Reid said, "There are so many things that indicate the truthfulness of that story that I can't disregard it."

He said that if Helen "was manufacturing a story, it would seem as though she would have made a very different kind of story."

He said "I don't believe her mind could conceive this course of conduct which she testified to as a matter of imagination."

"I was impressed," Reid said, "with the idea that she was too simple-minded to concoct that kind of story."

From a letter by Oscar Lee, warden of the Wisconsin State Prison, to the Marathon County Clerk of Courts, dated October 16, 1933:

Dear Sir:

Gumz was sentenced to this institution by your court on August 1, 1933, to serve 18 months for the crime of Statutory Rape, received August 1, 1933.

He was transferred to the Central State Hospital for the Insane, Waupun, Wisconsin, today.

Frank and Amanda Gumz had seven children. They lost their farm. Three years later, Gumz was killed in a car accident.

Some 45 years later, Kenny would tell investigators that he believed Clarence was his father.

It is possible, of course, that Gumz did rape Helen, and that he was Kenny's father. It is possible that he did not rape Helen, and that Clarence was Kenny's father. It is possible that Helen was sexually abused by both Gumz and Clarence. It is possible that neither man was Kenny's father.

Kenny could never be sure, really.

No one could, really.

Chapter 3

Small Yellow Bees

——— 1 ———

It was nearing 5 a.m. when Kenny turned his car left onto the rutted dirt driveway leading from West Townline Road to the front door of Clarence's house. He parked his car beside his camper, fished a couple of beers from a Styrofoam cooler resting on the floor of the back seat and, with a grunt, climbed out.

A little light had already begun leaking into the sky and the air was thick with the promise of rain. A couple of dogs came from around the corner of the house, looked at Kenny, then trotted into the woods.

Kenny yanked open the door to his camper and was setting the beers down on his kitchen counter when it struck him that he hadn't seen Randy's car parked in its usual place in front of the house. Kenny hunched down to peer through his window and saw that the kitchen light was on. He poked his head out his door. From somewhere in the house, Randy's new radio was on, turned up so high that even Kenny could hear it.

Arvin and Margaret Apfelbeck were not as young as they once were, but they still had the house to keep up and the farm to run and the cattle to tend, and if it took them a little longer to do things now, well then, that just meant they had to start the day a little earlier.

Neither minded a little hard work. Hard work was something Arvin and Margaret understood and respected.

By 5 a.m., Margaret had already cooked Arvin a little something to eat and was pulling on her boots, fixing to head out the back door and towards the barn, when she heard a car pull into the yard. She peered out her window and saw it was Kenny Kunz.

She flipped on the flood lights and opened the door, leaving the screen door between herself and Kenny.

"I need help," he said.

"You need help?" she asked. The Apfelbecks had lived less than a quarter of a mile from the Kunzes for decades, but other than a passing familiarity with Helen and Clarence, Margaret hardly knew the family at all. Now, here was Kenny, half-drunk and looking half-crazy and standing outside her door. She wished Arvin would hurry up.

"Kenny," she said.

"Randy's on the floor," Kenny said. "Blood all over. Clarence is in the bed. Marie."

Margaret could not make out what he was talking about. Kenny was frightening her.

"Where were you?"

"A party," Kenny said. "We have to call an ambulance."

"Now Kenny," Margaret said. "You have a phone down there at your place. Why didn't you call from there?"

"Wires cut. Outside of the house, the wires are cut."

Margaret told Kenny to stay were he was and went to find Arvin. A few minutes passed, and Arvin came to the door. Kenny told him he had just come home from a party and found Randy, Clarence and Marie dead.

"Call an ambulance," Kenny said.

Arvin opened the door and Kenny came into the kitchen. Margaret didn't care for it one bit.

"There's the phone," she said.

Kenny looked down.

"There's the phone, Kenny."

"Maybe he can't read," she thought. She looked up the Marathon County Sheriff's Department number and handed Kenny the phone book. Kenny didn't budge.

"Here, for God's sakes," Arvin said.

He took the book away from Kenny and called the Sheriff's number himself, told the dispatcher there had been some kind of accident out at the Kunzes' place on West Townline Road and that somebody needed to head on out there. No, he wasn't sure what had happened. Just some kind of accident. Yes. Yes. People injured. West Townline. Right. Thanks.

Margaret turned Kenny toward the door and told him to head on home, that the police would be there any minute and that he needed to wait for them there.

Kenny nodded. He stepped into the Apfelbecks' backyard. The sun was just up, but a cloud cover was soaking up all the light. A hornet hummed by Kenny's head. As Margaret was closing the door, he turned to her and said, "What a way to start my vacation."

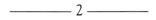

————— 2 —————

It was the morning after a dull night of patrol duty and Marathon County Sheriff's Deputy Steven E. Steppert was beginning to think about breakfast when the radio in his squad car came alive.

An accident west of Athens, on Townline Road. Didn't sound like a big deal, he thought. No need for sirens or lights. He drove east, toward the brightening sky. Looked like rain.

He listened to the chatter on police radio. The Athens Volunteer Fire Department had sent out three ambulances, and they had driven west along Townline Road clear into the next county and hadn't seen an accident.

They were turning around. Heading east now. Look. There's a man standing in the road. Waving us down. Geesh, Steppert thought. Silence on the radio. Then a frantic voice:

"This isn't an accident," the voice said. "Something terrible happened here. Where are the police?"

The moment Steppert drove into the Kunzes' driveway and saw all three ambulance attendants doing nothing but waiting in the yard he figured people were dead.

The attendants were talking to a fourth man—a short fellow in a blue wind-breaker and a gimme cap. They left him to talk to Steppert. The man stood almost motionless, except for a slight rocking motion at his hips and shoulders. He stood with his hands in his pockets, staring at the house.

"Who's that?" Steppert asked.

One of the attendants explained that that was Kenny Kunz, the guy who waved them into the yard. He's drunk, the attendant said. There are three stiffs in the house, he said. All kin. All appear to have been shot. Kenny says two women are missing.

In the shadows of the entry-way, in what appeared to be an enclosed porch, Steppert could make out the figure of a woman sitting on some steps beside an opened door. The attendant followed his eyes.

"Dead," he said.

Steppert spent four minutes in the house. He saw the woman on the step, a man on the kitchen floor, and a man in a bed in the living room. All had been shot in the head. The man in the kitchen looked like he had been smashed in the head with something. There were cats everywhere. The house smelled like cat piss, he thought. It smelled like dogs, too. There were a couple of other rooms to check, but Steppert had seen enough.

He couldn't breathe.

Kenny was still standing in the yard, looking toward the house, when Steppert picked his way pass the dead woman and made it back outside. He handed Kenny a Miranda Rights card.

"Okay. So you're Ken. What's your last name, Ken?"

Kenny looked away.

"Ken. Your last name."

"Kenny Kunz."

"Okay. We'll start at the top here, Ken. Okay, first of all, why don't you read that for me. This line here."

"You have the right to remain silent." Kenny read the line with ease, but in a whisper and without a trace of inflection. Steppert could smell his breath. Boozy.

"Okay," Steppert said. "Now, do you understand what that means? What does that mean to you?"

Kenny placed his chin against his shoulder and looked away.

"What does it mean to you, Ken?"

"I really don't understand it," Kenny said.

"Okay. Let's go over it again," Steppert said. "You have the right to remain silent. Do you know what the word 'silent' means?"

"Yeah."

"What does it mean?

"To be silent."

"Pardon?"

"To be silent."

"Silent. And what does that mean to you, Ken, if something is silent?"

"You don't say nothing."

"Okay. You have the right to remain silent. You have the right not to say anything. Okay. That means you don't have to say anything to me. You don't have to talk to me. Do you understand that? Now tell me what that means to you. Just the top line. 'You have the right to remain silent.' What does that mean to you?"

Kenny took his hands out of his pockets, then he put them back in.

"Don't have to say," Kenny said.

"Pardon?"

"Don't say nothing. Don't have to talk."

"Right, Ken. Right. You don't have to say anything. Okay. Do you understand that? You don't have to say anything to me."

It took Steppert a while to walk Kenny through the Miranda card. Then, under a section titled "Waiver of Rights," Steppert had Kenny sign his name. He also jotted down the time: 5:25 a.m.

"Okay," Steppert said. "Now you were here last night. Who was all at the house?"

"All were here."

Steppert was a big man. Heavy set. He moved slowly and by the book, keeping his emotions in check and his expressions hidden behind a thick black mustache. He was beginning to lose his patience.

"Okay. All. Who is all? Who do you mean by 'all?'"

"They were all here then. Clarence."

"Clarence is what—a relative of yours?"

Ken turned his head away.

"My dad."

"Your dad? Okay. Clarence was here. Who else was here?"

"And Helen."

"Okay, Helen. Who's Helen?"

Kenny grew upset. He rubbed his hand across his face, then looked toward the house. More sheriff's deputies were beginning to arrive.

"It's Clarence's sister."

"Your aunt. Helen would be your aunt?"

"My mother."

"Helen is your mother?"

Kenny looked at Steppert. Looked away. "Yeah."

"Clarence's wife then. Clarence and Helen are your parents?"

"Yeah."

"Okay. Who else was here?"

"Marie."

"Okay. Who's Marie?"

Kenny looked toward the woman on the steps. Tears formed at the edges of his eyes.

"She's laying over there."

"Is that a relative of yours?"

"Yeah. Um. My aunt."

"Okay, now, how would she be your aunt? Your mother's sister or your father's sister?"

Kenny paused for a long moment, looking for words.

"Ah, you know. See. They never married. Helen was my mother. And Clarence . . ."

"Was your father." Steppert did not see where Kenny was going. "Okay. Who is Marie?"

"My sister. No. It wouldn't be my sister. Let's figure . . ."

"What would Marie's last name be?"

"Kunz. All Kunz."

"So, okay, there was Clarence, Marie and Helen here last night. Anybody else?"

"Randy. Randy's on the floor over there."

"Randy is your brother?"

"Yes."

"Anybody else?"

"Irene. Irene is Helen's sister. That would be six of us altogether."

"Including you." Steppert had been jotting stuff into his notebook, trying to make out the relationships. He had drawn boxes around names, linking them with arrows to other boxes. It was an illegible scrawl.

"Right," he said. "Now, I see it's kind of crowded in that house—with six people living in it, it's kind of crowded. Kind of a small house, right?

"Okay, were there any arguments yesterday at all? Did Clarence and Randy, or Marie and Helen, did anybody get into an argument yesterday? Everybody was getting along pretty good?"

"Everything was okay when I left," Kenny said. "Everyone was eating supper. After a while they said—Randy and Helen says they was going to the Athens fireworks. 'Okay,' I says to them and I left. And that's all I know about it.

"See," Kenny said. "Helen and Irene are missing. And the car is missing. Randy's car is missing."

"Helen and Irene are missing," Steppert said. He looked at his notes. "Your mother and your aunt."

"I can't find Helen and Irene. And Randy's car is gone."

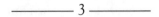

———— 3 ————

Detective Sergeant Randall Hoenisch and Sergeant Harvey Woodward were on their way home after spending the night working an undercover drug investigation in neighboring Taylor County when Steppert's request for a detective came over the radio. Both men sighed as Woodward turned the car toward toward Townline Road.

It was about 5:45 a.m. when they reached the Kunz farm. Three or four dogs came out of the woods to sniff them as they climbed out the squad. Hoenisch made a mental note to call the Humane Society. If there was a lot of blood, he didn't want the dogs getting into it.

Steppert filled them in: three bodies in the house—two men and a woman. All shot in the head. All related to each other, and to that guy over there. Ken Kunz. He's drunk. Says two women are missing. Both elderly. A car is missing too, he said.

Hoenisch looked over at Kenny, who still stood on the small patch of grass just outside the house.

One of the dogs sat on the ground beside him, leaning its head into his hip. Kenny swayed back and forth and gently rubbed the dog behind its ears. He took off his cap and rubbed his nose with the back of his sleeve, then fished some tissue out of his back pocket. He was crying.

"Come on," Hoenisch said to Woodward, and the two men walked toward the house.

Marie was wearing a loose-fitting dark blue and red printed blouse and a pair of blue polyester pants. She sat on the second of three steps leading into an enclosed porch that served as the house's only entrance. Her feet, which were shod in blue tennis shoes with white stripes, were planted on the bottom step, side by side in a girlish, almost prissy way.

Marie was less than 5 feet tall, and weighed about 85 pounds. As Hoenisch stooped to examine her wounds, she seemed to him to be no larger that a 10-year-old. Her hands were tiny and folded against her chest, her head bowed toward them as if in prayer.

Marie's body slumped to its left, so that her head rested on the floor in a puddle of blood. Flecks of blood stained her asphalt-colored hair.

She had been shot once, at the very top center of her right cheek and dry blood formed a ring around her swollen right eye, leaking down the crevices of her ancient face.

The blood on the floor came from an H-shaped exit wound at the back of Marie's head. The blood flowed between a chair and a pile of wood, forming an inch-deep pool in the northwest corner of the room.

Small yellow bees hovered over it.

Hoenisch stepped around Marie, crossed the enclosed porch and went through the opened door of the kitchen. A single bulb glared from an uncovered socket. The room felt over-exposed.

Randy's body lay on its back in the center of the floor, between a Formica-topped table and a wood cooking stove. His mouth was wide open and his eyes were fiercely shut, as if he had died squinting into the raw bulb hanging above his head. Blood was everywhere. Blood so fresh, it glittered.

Randy looked like he had been beaten up a bit before being shot.

His long thin face was bruised and there was a gash across his forehead. His left arm lay on the floor in a crazy angle. Hoenisch assumed it had been broken. There was a bullet hole in Randy's right temple and what looked like an exit wound at the back of his head at the base of the skull. His mouth was open, and a fly crawled along his teeth.

Randy's red and white checkered shirt was soaked with blood and there were drops of blood dotting his jeans. He was wearing the same kind of running shoes as Marie: blue with white stripes.

Hoenisch glanced at Randy's hands. They also were like Marie's, small and delicate. Dirty, though. With the finger nails bitten to the quick.

Hoenisch stood up and waved away the flies. There was a shell casing on the floor, .22-caliber, near the stove. A radio blared country music from on top of the refrigerator and a clay-colored cat jumped onto a chair.

Hoenisch whispered: "Get!"

Hoenisch reached to turn the radio off, then decided to leave it on. He stepped into the living room. It was as dusky as the kitchen had been bright, with the light from the kitchen thinning to a yellow murkiness by the time it reached the far wall.

Hoenisch stood in the doorway and waited for his eyes to adjust to the half-darkness. A few moments, and the shapes that seemed to fill the room became recognizable objects: the rectangle to his right became a metal file cabinet, in front of him was a chair, and a box, and a fold-up bed that was still folded up. There was a pot on the floor beside the fold-up bed, and a vile looking muck inside the pot.

A grey cat moved between a stack of boxes, and another cat jumped onto a table. More shelves. A bed in the center of the room. Boxes. Bags of trash. Another cat. No, maybe that was a dog. More boxes. Hoenisch picked his way around the objects till he reached the bed that contained Clarence's body.

Clarence looked like he had been shot twice in the face—once in the right cheek, just below the right temple, and once just below the center of his right eye.

The barrel of the gun—small caliber, maybe a .22—had been held right up to him, almost touching his skin, and the two blasts left circles of gun powder burns around the bullet holes. His right eye was open and his left eye was closed.

Hoenisch figured the old man had been asleep and that the force of the gunshot blew his right eye lid open.

Blood leaked from the bullet hole beneath the old man's temple, pooled in his ears, then trickled onto the pillow, onto the bed and onto the floor, where it formed a small puddle that surrounded a pair of bent and cracked shoes.

About a foot away from the top of the bed, leaning against the wall, was an old rifle. It was a .22-caliber.

Although the room was cluttered mess, Hoenisch decided that it didn't look like it had been ransacked. It had a kind of crazy order to it—sort of a consistent lunacy that had not been disturbed.

It was as if the people who lived here didn't know how to discern the essential from the non-essential, trash from treasure, spoiled from fresh. Everything was saved, stored in bags and boxes or simply stacked in piles, some of which appeared not to have been altered in years.

Hoenisch pushed open the door that led from the living room into Kenny's old room. It was clearly no longer used for anything more than storage. There was a desk in the room, with an opened drawer containing several brown envelopes filled with money. Lots of money.

All that money in plain view and no apparent attempt to ransack the place. Hoenisch had to question robbery as a motive for the killings.

He was eager to get back outside and have a talk with Kenny, but as he walked back into the kitchen, he noticed the blood that leaked from Randy's head and spread across the worn wood floor flowed toward a doorway partially blocked by the wood stove and an overstuffed chair.

The detective stepped around the chair, which had been turned with its back toward the kitchen, and walked into the room. There he made a discovery that virtually eliminated Kenny as a suspect.

Another body.

It was Irene's body, though Hoenisch, of course, didn't know it was Irene.

All he knew was that Kenny had reported finding three bodies in the house and two old women missing.

And here was one of the old women, sitting in the overstuffed chair, holding an opened Hitchcock Mystery Magazine in her lap.

She had been shot at least once in the back of the head.

God, did she look spooky: She wore a brown babushka and a black cardigan sweater, a blue and purple striped dress and, despite the July heat, leather stockings and black snowmobile boots.

Her left eye was black and blue, and the cheek below it was grotesquely swollen. Blood flowed down her neck, across her left shoulder and down the front of her dress.

What was spooky about her was her size. So tiny. Maybe 4 foot 10 inches. Maybe 95 pounds. A little old woman. Shot in the back of the head.

Hoenisch thought: All right. You just don't make a mistake about how many people in your family you just executed.

So, if Kenny killed these people, he would have to be lying. He would have had to devise a plan in which he shot these four, apparently disposed of the fifth, removed his brother's car, then told investigators that two of the five victims were missing—when actually one of the two was still at the crime scene—just to make it look like he didn't do it.

Hoenisch thought: Kenny was either innocent, or damn near the smartest killer he had ever encountered.

He went to find out.

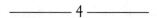

———— 4 ————

Kenny was still standing on the lawn, virtually in the same spot, when Hoenisch emerged from the house. He walked over to Kenny, and the first thing he noticed when he got there was the blood on the front of Kenny's jacket.

A whole new set of suspicions set in. But if Kenny was smart enough to pretend he only saw three bodies in the house, then surely he would have been smart enough to wipe the blood off his coat.

"Kenny, right? I'm Detective Hoenisch."

Kenny glanced down at Hoenisch's blue jeans, then up at his mustache and long curly hair.

"Now, Kenny. You told Deputy Steppert there are two people missing. Who is missing?"

"Helen and Irene. And the car is missing."

Hoenisch decided to let it go for a minute. He'd come back.

"I see. What kind of car is missing?"

" '75 Oldsmobile. Randy's car. Purple with, ah, purple with a dark top. Kind of maroon."

"Two door? All right. Who would be driving it if Randy's not driving it."

"I don't know."

"Do you have other relatives in the area?"

"No."

"Kenny, is there anybody that would have come here last night to visit that you would be aware of?"

"I don't think so."

"So Irene is missing. Could Irene drive a car?"

"No."

"Who else is missing?"

"Helen."

"Could Helen drive a car?"

"No."

"Neither of them could drive a car?"

Kenny shook his head. Hoenisch was all but ready to dismiss Kenny as a suspect. If Kenny had killed them, then the only reason he would have gotten rid of Randy's car would have been to make it appear that the missing woman had committed the crime, then used the car as a getaway vehicle. Now he says the missing woman can't drive.

"What time did you get here this morning?" Hoenisch asked.

"Five."

"About 5 o'clock this morning? Tell me what happened."

Kenny told him about spending the night in Milan and about leaving the cheese factory and about coming home and noticing Randy's car missing and the light on in the kitchen.

"Then I see Marie laying there," Kenny said. "The door was open."

"You see Marie laying by the porch. Then what?"

"I went in. I seen Randy." Kenny's voice grew quieter. He placed his chin against his shoulder and looked down.

"Randy was in the kitchen. Then I walked over, and Clarence was laying in bed."

"Clarence was laying in bed."

"Then I—next thing I did was, I tried the telephone, but the telephone didn't work so I quick went down by Arvin."

Hoenisch wondered why Kenny didn't check the other room. It was obviously a bedroom. Clarence had been shot in bed. Two people unaccounted for. Why didn't Kenny look for them in other bedroom? Why did he assume they were missing?

"Arvin," Hoenisch said.

"I told him what happened—call the police or something. I didn't know what to do."

"Irene's what—in her 70s? You can't find Irene. And who else can't we find?"

"Helen."

"And neither Helen nor Irene could drive a car, right?
Kenny nodded.

"Where would Randy's car be?"

"I don't know."

Hoenisch asked Kenny about the rifle near Clarence's bed.
Kenny said it hadn't been fired in 20 years. He said it was the only gun
the family owned. The detective was about to press Kenny on the
missing car when an investigator came up and snapped a picture of
Kenny's shoes. Kenny shimmied back, away from the camera, and the
investigator took a picture of the spot where he just stood.

Kenny became tense. Hoenisch wished they could have waited.

"What he's doing, Ken, is—because there's been a crime in the
house—he's got to take pictures of all our foot prints, all our shoes, so
we can say we were authorized to be in that house.

"He's even going to take pictures of the sheriff's foot—so that's
no problem. He took mine, yours, all the ambulance drivers'."

The sheriff Hoenisch was referring to—LeRoy E. Schillinger—
had just arrived and was being briefed.

Schillinger had been sheriff for just over six months, and
Hoenisch wasn't sure what to make of him. It wasn't that Schillinger
was green exactly—almost 50, Schillinger had been the small town of
Stratford's chief of police for 16 years.

It was just that Schillinger, though seemingly well-intentioned,
was kind of a rube. And he had a big mess on his hands. The previous
sheriff, Louis Gianoli, had left a demoralized department facing a
John Doe investigation by the district attorney's office. The mistrust
between the various factions of the department was virtually systemic.

A lot of the rank-and-file officers were taking a wait-and-see
approach to the new management. They wanted to see if he could
bring the department under his control.

Schillinger walked up. Kenny stared at the gun strapped to
his waist.

"This is Sheriff LeRoy Schillinger, Kenny," Hoenisch said.

Schillinger took Kenny's hand and shook it. Kenny looked a little overwhelmed. Hoenisch decided to press Kenny about the car again.

"Kenny, where do you think Randy's car is?"

"I don't know," Kenny said.

Kenny was explaining that Randy always left the keys to his car under the dash, when Schillinger interrupted.

"Does Randy have a girlfriend?"

"No," Kenny said.

Hoenisch wasn't sure where the sheriff was going with the question. It didn't seem like he had a follow-up.

Hoenisch waited a moment, then asked, "Has any neighbors stopped in lately? Has any of the neighbors stopped in?"

"Well, they don't . . . uh, neighbors, no they don't stop. Not too often."

Schillinger moved in a little closer.

"But you were here last night, is that right?" Schillinger asked.

Kenny looked frightened.

"You left, what—about seven, isn't that what you've already told me?" Hoenisch asked.

Schillinger ignored the signal.

"Was Randy here then?" Schillinger asked.

"Everybody was here," Hoenisch answered. Schillinger looked at Hoenisch for a moment and smiled. Then he looked at Kenny.

"Yeah," Kenny said. "Everything was okay."

"Who's in the kitchen? Who is the younger person in the kitchen?" Schillinger asked.

"Randy," Kenny said.

"That's who?"

"Randy."

The sheriff looked stumped. He obviously had been nursing some kind of theory, and the theory just went south.

"That's Randy," Schillinger said.

He put his hands on his hips, smiled suddenly, and backed away.

Hoenisch continued to work Kenny over, with Schillinger quiet and just listening in.

Kenny told them that when he had left the house, shortly after 7 p.m., he went to till the family garden, located down a dirt road about a quarter of a mile north of the house, and that he had worked the garden until it started getting dark.

He also lied to them. Afraid he could get fired if investigators told his boss he had been drinking, he told them he had gone to the cheese factory to work on some pumps.

"Kenny," Hoenisch said. "Do you have any idea what happened to Clarence and Randy and Marie?"

"I don't know."

"I mean . . . what do you *think* happened to them?"

"They shot them."

"They *shot* them?"

Hoenisch voice sounded a little too eager. Kenny backed away.

"I don't know."

"You know," Hoenisch said, "we don't either. You know they are deceased."

"I know," Kenny said.

"They have passed away, so we haven't looked at the bodies to see what caused their death. But you think they were shot?"

"I don't know."

"I mean, what do you think? What's the first thing when you seen Marie, what was the first thing that entered your head?"

"Well, she was laying there and getting old and I figured maybe something happened to her." Kenny started to cry.

"And when I walked in there and found the rest. Randy was laying there. Then I picked up the phone and I couldn't get through the phone so I went down by the neighbor and he called."

"Okay, Kenny," Hoenisch said softly. "All right."

He waited for Kenny to stop crying, then he said: "Do you have any idea, Kenny, who did this?"

"No."

"No idea."

"No idea at all."

"Kenny. If I asked you a point blank question, would you tell me the truth?"

Kenny nodded.

"Did you kill them people in the house?"

"No."

"You didn't."

"No."

"Do you have any idea who did?"

"No, I don't," Kenny said. "Don't know."

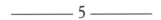

————— 5 —————

From an investigative report, filed by Detective Rick Schroeder, concerning his search of Kenny Kunz's trailer:

The trailer was littered fully with old discarded garbage, including empty beer cans, empty bean and soup cans, half eaten sandwiches, old cheese, and a variety of meats.

The decaying food left a stench on the interior of the trailer that would make it almost uninhabitable to an individual. Along with discarded garbage, there were areas of maggot and ant activity, also several live rodents were observed during this search.

It should be noted that other items found in the trailer were new items that had never been opened, a sampling of which is: new electrical devices, radios, electric frying pans, corn poppers, a variety of tools, electrical tools, and a variety of hardware items. It was apparent these items had been purchased, simply placed in the trailer and forgotten, and never used after that point.

I located an uncashed payroll check from the end of June pay period, which would indicate that Ken Kunz was probably occupying the trailer at the end of June.

The following items of evidence were removed from the trailer house: 41 porno books, including Hustler, Penthouse, Playboy, and hard pornographic magazines with various names; blood stained white tissue papers found lying on the bed mixed in with the blankets and other materials. Also removed was a large gross pack of fireworks.

It didn't take investigators very long to find Randy's car.

It was abandoned on a dirt road just behind the Kunzes' vegetable garden. Kenny had told Hoenisch that before he had gone into Milan, he had spent a couple of hours rototilling the garden, and Hoenisch decided it was time for another chat.

He found Kenny still standing on the little patch of grass near the house, watching in what appeared to be utter dismay as squad car after squad car, as well as trucks from the State Crime Laboratory, the coroner's office, the Athens Fire Department and the Humane Society, formed a line on the unpaved road in front of the Kunzes' farmhouse.

People walked back and forth, passing Kenny as if he were invisible, as if he had no mass, no gravitational pull. Sometimes, it seemed, they walked right through him, as if he possessed no more substance than shade.

"Kenny," Hoenisch said. "You could really help us out. Let me ask you this. If we could find Randy's car, see, we might really get a start on figuring out what happened."

Kenny was quiet. Then he said, "I don't know know where it is. Randy's car."

"Yeah. I know you don't. But where would you guess. I mean, if you were to just guess—guess, okay?—where would you guess it was?"

Kenny shrugged.

But he also looked north.

Hoenisch caught the look, and it made his heart sink a little. He really wanted to believe Kenny hadn't killed anybody.

"Come on. Just guess. I want you to guess, Kenny."

Kenny paused, then said, "Up the road." He tossed his head just a fraction, gesturing toward the garden.

"Yes. Up the road," Hoenisch said. He crossed his arms and cocked his head and toed a gray clod of dried mud.

"Why would you guess up the road, Kenny?." "I don't know."
"Why up the road, Kenny?"

It was getting hot, and though his face was streaked with sweat, Kenny still had not removed his wind-breaker, still had not unfastened the top button of his shirt, still had not lifted back his cap.

That bothered Hoenisch.

"Why?"

"The other guys were talking about it," Kenny said. "I heard them talking about finding Randy's car."

Hoenisch didn't know what to make of that.

"Jesus, Kenny," he said. "Why don't you take your coat off?"

From an investigative report, filed by Detective Sergeant Harold Bean:

After arriving at the crime scene, we were instructed to process the crime scene near the garden area where Randy Kunz's car had been located. The reason for processing this area as quickly as possible was due to the possibility of rain.

Later into the afternoon, Sea Scouts were obtained and, along with detective personnel, they attempted to search the area of the Kunzes' property. This search provided negative results.

Detective Johnson and I spoke to Kenneth Kunz later that afternoon, at length, regarding the situation. We took him back to the garden area, where he informed us that the tracks leading into the garden were not there when he left the evening before after rototilling.

At this time, more impressions were taken of the tire tracks in the immediate area of the garden.

After the crime lab was finished with their collection of evidence regarding the bodies, they were later removed from the residence.

The bodies were transported to Wausau Hospital for x-rays and from there transferred to Madison for autopsies.

It was almost dark before the bodies were removed and Schillinger started letting some of the deputies go home.

"Tomorrow," he told them. "Bright and early. We're going to find this Helen woman."

Night, and the temperature dropped into the 50s and Hoenisch, who had hardly slept in days, began to shiver. The cooling air adhered to his skin, and his skin felt like a thing that had been wrapped around him. Hidebound, he watched the bodies carried out on stretchers from the battered home. He thought about their tiny hands.

Chapter 4

Sifting Through
the Residue

— 1 —

From autopsy report W87–271:

> *This is Dr. (Robert) Huntington dictating at 8:48 a.m. on July 6, 1987, in the presence of Coroner John Larson of Marathon County.*
>
> *Initial notification about this uproar was received by me when Mr. Alberts called yesterday afternoon to relate that they had at that time four bodies from a homicide incident in Marathon County. A fifth missing person has yet to be located.*
>
> *As per request of coroner, we will start with our 87–271, Randy Kunz.*
>
> *The body is that of a somewhat gaunt-appearing thin Caucasian male reasonable as late 20s or thereabouts in age. Scalp hair is brown and bloodied. Coroner Larson's attention is immediately directed to a wound angling from about midline upper forehead down into medial right eyebrow.*
>
> *This will have to be studied further.*
>
> *Blood streaks from this over to the left side of the face, and some also streaks down over the right side of the nose.*

Blood is in the mouth, but not particularly obvious inside the nose. Examination of the left upper arm shows a fracture in the middle of this, not at all subtle, with blood extending around it.

There is blood coming onto the thighs of anterior pants, especially left. The blood on the right pants thigh is more in the medial aspect. Large drop pattern with tracks from above to below on the pants is present over the anterior left thigh.

From a list of items removed from the Kunzes' farmhouse on July 6 by Marathon County Sheriff Deputies:

Ten envelopes, nine of which are brown and indicate a direct deposit for social security money, and one which is blue and white and shows the insignia for GTE. Each envelope contains coins, currency and checks. The money totals $4,196.

Five purses from the northwest room, containing a total of $5,125.73.

One plastic container from the northwest storage room containing two marbles and $27.29.

One LaCrosse shoe box containing Christmas decorations, envelopes with mail dated 1984 and 1986, and $230.

One wallet containing $25 and five pictures of Randy Kunz.

One gunshot wound is identified in the back of left neck at a level 2 and ¼ inches back of, and roughly ⅜ inches below, a level of lower attachment of left ear.

A laceration with abrasion is found in the left periental scalp. The laceration starts back behind the left ear and angles forward and right toward the median forehead.

A second gunshot wound is found ½ inch above the the upper level of attachment of right external ear. This area is shaved, revealing a lacerated wound with hemorrhage around it.

A probe is inserted into the wound and the wound tract heads downward. This is a close, but not contact, entry wound.

One paper bag containing assorted currency envelopes and a wallet that holds several papers and three savings passbooks from the Athens Bank. The currency totals $1,636.87. The bag also contains an uncashed Homestead refund check to Clarence in the amount of $724, and three uncashed social security checks for Marie, Helen and Irene, each in the amount of $442.34. There is another uncashed social security check for Clarence for $154.

One brown paper bag containing papers dating back to the late 1970s, a 7-year-old check made out to Clarence for $1.14 and $536.49 in cash.

One paper bag containing a check, made out to Clarence, for $1.63.

One paper bag containing $3.40 in loose coins.

One brown paper bag containing a red pocketbook and a black wallet. They are new, are still in their boxes, and they contain $36.04.

The body is undressed, revealing feces in the underwear. The relatively clean shoes are removed, revealing filthy socks and then some of the dirtiest feet ever seen here.

A gunshot wound of entry is located in the lateral left upper arm, 5 and ¼ inches below the top of shoulder. The arm at this location is extremely distorted, and a comminuted fracture of the humerus is noted on X-ray, along with fragments of metal.

Closer examination of the wound of the forehead reveals a 1 and ¾ by ³/₁₆ inch defect which angles from midline upper forehead down and laterally towards the right eyebrow. It has a blackish floor and a dry abraded edge, with small skin tags pointing inferiorly.

This indicates a gunshot graze wound, with the bullet traveling caudad to cephalad.

One envelope containing $11 and, laying beneath it, a $1 bill.

One red wallet containing $67.86.

One plastic container containing $26 and one safety pin.

Six containers, filled with coupons, paper clips and $23.44 in loose cash and change.

One filing cabinet box containing old medical bills, envelopes and pouches. The envelopes and pouches contain $2,244 in cash.

The body measures 65 and ½ inches and weighs an estimated 110 lbs. The hair is dark brown and is distributed in a normal adult male pattern, with some frontal alopecia.

The teeth are all present, but are in poor repair.

A generous amount of dirt covers the entire frontal surface of the body. Multiple healed and healing purplish-brown scars measuring up to 1.0 cm in diameter are scattered over the volar aspect of the arms, both flanks, entire back, buttocks and upper thighs.

The feet are extremely dirty. The nails of the feet are untrimmed and dirty. The fingernails appear to have been chewed or trimmed about as far back as possible.

One brown paper bag containing numerous papers belonging to Clarence, many of them going back to the 1920s. One is a birth certificate for Clarence. Another is an envelope marked "important papers." In it are three $1 bills.

One brown paper bag containing the birth records of Randy and Kenny. One cardboard matchbox containing $80.

One paper bag containing loose change and currency, as well as a black purse containing coins. The money in the bag and purse totals $247.37.

Two brown purses containing $40.42.

The gunshot wound of entry above the right ear came in through the skull in the temporal region. The bullet created extensive fracturing around the right petrous ridge, but coursed through the right temporal lobe and then through the right cerebellar hemisphere. It creased across a ridge in the occipital bone and left a fragment of soft metal.

The bullet then exited the skull in the left posterior fossa and came down through the neck to the exit wound noted.

One cardboard box containing 18 jars and cans, two purses, one shoe-box and a plastic bowl. The purses and shoe-box contain $302.87.

A brown paper bag containing a plastic bowl and an envelope. The bowl holds change, the envelope holds cash. Total: $50.56.

Thirty-five jars and five plastic containers, all filed with cash and loose change. Total: $1,324.12.

The body is opened with a Y-shaped incision to reveal organs in their usual places. Very little subcutaneous fat is present at the umbilicus.

The heart weighs 200 gm. The heart is dissected in the direction of blood flow, to reveal normal valves and chambers.

The larynx is opened in situ to reveal no blood.

The stomach contains small amounts of pinkish fluid.

The liver weighs 1,000 gm and has a pale surface.

The bladder contains a large amount of clear yellow urine, approximately 600 ml.

The fresh brain weight is 1,400 gm. It is fixed in formalin for complete dissection at a later date.

One envelope containing $120.

A brown paper bag containing $1.65 in loose change.

A brown bag containing numerous envelopes stuffed with cash and one worn white vinyl purse, also containing cash and documents dating from the late 1970s. Cash in this bag totals $3,582.07.

Final diagnoses:
1. Gunshot, very close range, right temporal region, with penetration of right temporal lobe and cerebellum, with exit wound left posterior neck near base of skull.
2. Gunshot, left lateral upper arm, with comminuted fracture.
3. Graze gunshot, right forehead.
4. Blunt injury laceration, left scalp.
5. Moderate fatty metamorphosis and periportal fibrosis, liver, suggestive of alcohol abuse.

From a Marathon County Sheriff's Department report filed by Detective Phillip R. Johnson:

The total amount of money recovered from the Clarence Kunz residence is $20,418.14.

This includes all currency, coin, and check, except for the Homestead refund check to Clarence Kunz in the amount of $724.00, a social security check for Marie Kunz in the amount of $442.34, a social security check for Helen Kunz in the amount of $444.72, a social security check for Irene Kunz in the amount of $444.72, and a social security check in the amount of $154 addressed to Clarence Kunz.

Total amount of the above mentioned checks is $2,205.78. This is not included in the $20,418.14 grand total.

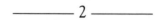

——— 2 ———

From autopsy report W87–272:

This is Dr. Huntington dictating in the presence of Coroner John Larson of Marathon County. This decedent is identified as Clarence Kunz.

The body is removed as is revealed to be that of an elderly, somewhat gaunt, Caucasian male. As currently received, the body is dressed in a bloody blue long-sleeved shirt, bags on the hands, undershirt and under-pants. No other garments are present.

The features immediately coming into view are two quite close rang gunshot wounds of the face. In the right cheek is a 1/8 by 1/8 gunshot wound of entry. Powder grains surround this wound for an even larger area, but are also distributed forward of the actual point of entry.

Abundant blood is present in the right ear.

Another gunshot wound of entry is just below the mid-right eye. Some powder particles go up onto the right side of the nose and the right upper lip. Abundant blood also emerges from the left external ear.

One brown paper bag containing two packages addressed to Randy. One package contains a pocket book entitled "Kama Sutra" and a white envelope with black and blue trim entitled "Your Erotic Love Notes from Adam," and three VHS cassettes featuring the following films: "Heather and the Bunny," "Around the World," "Beyond Arousal," "Diva Does the Director," "Throbbing Threesomes," and "Hot Wives."

The second contains a booklet, entitled "Bedside Companion," and two videocassettes: "Lesbian Lovers," and "Seeka Sex-Travanganza."

The body measured at 66 inches. What scalp hair there is is dark and gray, with almost a natural tonsure effect. The face is unshaven, and has been that way for at least one to three weeks.

A prominent skin tag is just above the left lateral mustache, and some smaller skin tags are present in that area.

The back of the shirt and the back of the undershirt are soaked with blood.

Looking down the abdomen shows some vein prominence pattern indicating early decomposition.

Undressing the body reveals normal hair distribution on the chest and abdomen and a very prominent right inguinal hernia with green decomposition.

Examination of the hands shows that the fingernails are poorly kept, and the interosseus muscles between the metacarpals are somewhat atrophied.

One brown paper bag containing two packages. One is addressed to H. Kunz, contains two videocassettes featuring: "Stud Wars," "Perfection," "Beverly Hills Cox," "Blonde Heat," "Candy Strippers II," "Lust on the Orient Express," "Deep Inside Vanessa Del Rio," "Project Ginger," "Delivers in the Rear," "Yank My Doodle," "Snake Eyes," "Burlex," and "The Next Best Thing."

The second package is addressed to Randy and contains a calendar: "Kisses 1987."

Roughly 50 gm of subdural blood is recovered from the left posterior head. Also recovered is one flattened bullet, just sitting there on the dura. Another bullet remnant is recovered from the left parieto-occipital area.

His bones cut with rather singular ease, especially ribs, and his skull appears to have more of an erythematous appearance on the inner table, from something going on in the marrow that is absolutely normal.

One brown paper bag containing a manila mailing envelope containing a videocassette, with the brand-name "Playmates," featuring the movie "Playoffs."

The body is opened with a Y-shaped incision to reveal 2 cm of fat at the umbilicus. The anterior rib cage is grossly unremarkable. The organs are found in their usual positions, with postmortem changes visible on their surfaces.

The esophageal is grossly unremarkable. The stomach is practically devoid of contents.

The splenic artery is extremely tortuous and averages 0.8 in diameter. The walls show calcification and several plaques occluding up to 50% of the lumen.

Brain weight at this examination is 1,175 gm.

The dura and sagittal sinus are unremarkable. Arachnoids are basically unremarkable, except for two grooving paths of gunshot wound in which the arachnoid is disrupted.

Several cartons containing adult magazines, and a brown paper bag containing Randy's old driver's license, as well as a Playgirl pocket calendar.

Final Diagnoses:
1. Gunshot, two, below right eye and anterior to right ear.
    A. Skull fractures, bilateral.
    B. Penetration of brain and transection of pons-medulla junction.
    C. Fragments of two bullets recovered.
2. Atherosclerosis, moderate to severe.
    A. Left mainstream coronary artery, 40% occlusion.
    B. Abdominal aorta, moderate.
    C. Splenic artery, severe.
3. Subendocardial fibrosis, focal, heart.
4. Apical pleural fibrosis, right lung.
5. Benign nodular hypertrophy, prostate.
6. Right inguinal hernia, reducible, large.
7. Early decomposition.

──────── 3 ────────

From autopsy report W87–273:

Dr. Huntington dictating on 6 July 1987 in the presence of Coroner John Larson of Marathon County. This body is identified to us only as Marie and is also identified as the body from the porch.

As received, this body is of an elderly Caucasian female with some curvature of the back. The body is dressed with a loose fitting print shirt, blue fabric pants, stockings and shoes. Removal of stockings and shoes reveals an extraordinary collection of dirt.

Studying the head shows a number of injuries. The actual gunshot wound of entry is at a level about ¼ of an inch below the mid-right lower eyelid.

A corresponding exit wound is identified on the back of the head in a very low occipital level at about two inches to left of midline.

A roughly H-shaped laceration array, well separate from both entry and exit, is present in the right back of the head.

One intact package containing 1,280 Thunder Bomb firecrackers.

Sixty-seven packages, each containing 16 Thunder Bomb firecrackers.

Four 8-shot, star-shaped Roman Candles.

Two packages of Air Travel with Report rockets.

Two Phoenix Flyers.

One Jumping Wheel.

One Saturn Missiles Battery 25 Shots.

Three Sky Rockets.

After the body is unclothed, it is further inspected. It is measured at 4 feet 11 and ½ inches and would be, quite reasonably, estimated as weighing on the order of 85 pounds.

The scalp hair is dark and gray with considerable blood in it. Abundant fly eggs are present around the bullet wound below the right globe, and the right globe itself is collapsed. Some blood is in the nose and mouth.

There appears to be a bruise in the upper lip.

The neck appears scrawny and somewhat bulging all at the same time. There is dirt in the fingernails. Hands are fairly small.

The feet are reasonable candidates as the dirtiest feet yet seen in this autopsy room. The curling thickened toenails are certainly champion, at least in my experience. Old fashioned underwear is present.

Examination of the back shows a dowager's hump, but not much else.

One box of Aircraft Carrier fireworks.

Three Sky Bloom Rockets.

Two Willow Rockets.

Three Color Silk Rockets.

Six boxes of gold sparklers.

One Garden of Innumerable Flowers.

Four packages, each containing 100 Big Apple firecrackers.

The scalp is reflected and the skull is opened to reveal that the bullet came across into the skull and entered the cranial vault just back of the sella turcia and to left of the midline.

The bullet creased across the pons medulla junction and created a very effective distribution there as well as to the left cerebellar hemisphere. It then exited the skull in the left occipital area as noted.

Abundant fractures are located around this exit hole. Abundant blood is present in the head.

Three Hot Stuff Cones.

Two Comets.

One Horal Shell.

One jar of M80 Cherry Bombs.

Two Ariel Flash Rockets.

One Wild Rocket.

Ten sticks of Punk.

Two M–90s.

The body is opened with a Y-shaped incision to reveal the organs in their usual positions.

Each lung weighs 260 gm. There are no obstructive vascular lesions. Cut sections show minimal anthracotic pigmentation. There is an irregular area of apical scarring in a patching distribution over an area 5 cm in diameter.

One box of Rio Snappers.

Three Champagne Party Poppers.

Thirty-eight smoke bombs.

Two green paper tanks.

One Opening Flower and Happy Bird.

One Dancing Butterfly.

Two boxes of Pop-Pop Snappers.

Brain weight at this examination is 1,075 gm. The left lower pons and medulla area have been basically blown apart.

One four-pack of Baby Magic Blooms.

Sixteen Colorful Birds.

Three Four-Seasons Flowers.

One Violets Crimson.

One box of glow worms.

Two Butterflies Welcome Spring.

Five Flying Whistle Helicopters.

> Final diagnoses:
> 1. Gunshot, close range, below right eye.
>   A. Collapse of right globe.
>   B. Destruction of brain at pons-medulla level with penetration of left cerebellum.
>   C. Exit wound left occiput.
> 2. Blunt injury laceration, scalp, right superior aspect.
>   A. Hairline fracture, 1.5 cm, outer table of skull.
>   B. Inner table of skull intact.
> 3. Apical scarring, right lung.
> 4. Histological changes suggestive of bronchial asthma.
> 5. Paratubal cyst, 5 cm, right side.
> 6. Cholelithiasis.

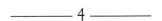

—————— 4 ——————

From autopsy report W87-274:

Dr. Huntington dictating 6 July 1987. This our 87-274. The body is identified as that of Irene Kunz.

This elderly lady, reported as age 81, is dressed in a babushka, brown and stained with blood.

A defect is in the right side of the babushka and below the ear, and in a corresponding position is identified as a gunshot wound. By identifying a couple of pieces of powder particle, we identify this as a gunshot wound of entry.

Two American Rifleman magazines, one dated September 1983 and the other dated January 1985.

One .22-caliber rifle, bolt action Springfield. Very rusty.

One .12-gauge shotgun, single-shot. Very rusty.

Review further under the babushka unfortunately shows another gunshot wound just about over the thyroid cartilage. This also has some abrasion, but it may be a wound of exit. Further study of the pronounced ecchymosis around the left eye shows that at the lower end of this is another gunshot wound. Another gunshot wound of entry is identified on the back occiput.

This lady, then, was shot at least twice.

The body is rolled over onto the face, and the wound of the back is studied. In addition to some abrasion around this occipital wound, there are fine particles of powder identified in the hair here. A review of the face wound shows that it is more lacerated.

She was therefore shot in the back of the head, and the exit is on the face.

A brown mailing envelope, addressed to Helen Kunz, containing a National Rifle Association belt buckle that says, "Vote Gun Rights."

A brown paper bag containing NRA materials.

The body is measured at 4'10" or 4'11" and would be estimated to weigh somewhere between 95 and 115 lbs. She does have a couple of centimeters of panniculus on the abdomen, but most of the protuberance is from gas. The scalp hair is sparse and dark and has a good deal of blood in it. Groinfolds are quite dirty, and so are the lower legs.

The toenails are markedly thick and dirty, though not to the extreme degree of the previous autopsy.

One brown paper bag containing a cardboard box used for holding wooden matches. Inside the box are three partially filled boxes of .22 shells. One box contains hollow points, one contains .22 longs and the third contains .22 long rifle shells.

The bullet entering the back of the head is in fact confirmed as that by the flare on the inside of the occipital bone and the dark rim around the point of outer table entry. This bullet then traversed the occipital lobe down through the cerebellum anteriorly across the cerebral peduncle and into the sella tursica area, where it smashed through and came out in the left eye region.

The fluid removed from the left eye is somewhat bloody. Internal neck dissection confirms the track direction of the neck shot from back to front.

One paper bag containing several "Alfred Hitchcock Mystery Magazines."

Some blood is down the airways, but not enough to drown her.

One brown paper bag containing National Rifle Association materials.

The body is opened with a T-shaped incision across the clavicles and down the midline to reveal organs in their usual places.

The heart weighs 240 gm.

Dissection of the coronary arteries reveals moderate atherosclerosis, with 30% occlusion of the left mainstream coronary artery, focal 70% occlusions of the left anterior descending and first diagonal coronary arteries, up to 25% occlusion of the circumflex coronary artery focally, and no significant occlusion of the right coronary artery.

One brown paper bag containing National Rifle Association materials.

Brain weight at this examination is 1,160 gm. Examination of the dura shows a somewhat shredded dura with unremarkable sagittal sinus. Examination of the brain itself shows a penetrating hole in the right occipital region.

Cut surfaces of the cerebrum reveal extensive subarachnoid hemorrhage. No definite contusions are identified in the frontal lobes.

Analysis is somewhat confused by some postmortem decomposition gas formation in the center of the brain.

One plastic bag containing one empty Pabst Blue Ribbon beer can, partially crushed with what appears to be several bullet holes, possibly .22-caliber.

Final diagnosis:
1. Gunshot wound to the head.
   A. Entry right occiput and exit under right eye.
   B. Penetration of occipital brain, cerebellum and cerebral penduncle.
   C. Inhalation of some blood.
2. Gunshot wound of right neck, without penetration of major structures.
3. Moderately severe coronary and aortic atherosclerosis.
4. Myocardial fibrosis, focal.
5. Moderate decomposition.
6. Chronic inflammation with dystrophic calcification, bladder.
7. Cholelithiasis.
8. Thyroid atrophy.

Part II

HELEN

Dust is the only Secret—
Death, the only One
You cannot find out all about

Emily Dickinson

Chapter *1*

Ashes to Ashes

————— 1 —————

Few things possess the power to churn a stomach quite like the smell emitted by a cheese factory dumpster on a hot summer's day: It is the aroma of turned milk, clotted waste, baked by-products, active bacteria. It is the stench of wholesomeness gone sour.

It was Monday, July 6th. A new dumpster had been placed beside the old dumpster behind the cheese factory in Milan, and the old dumpster had been sealed with strips of yellow plastic tape marked "Caution. Marathon County Sheriff's Department. Caution."

A man in his early 50s—grey mustache, thinning grey hair—fished a small folding knife from the right pocket of his baggy khaki pants and slit the yellow tape. He lifted the steel lid, letting it swing on its hinges and clang against the dumpster's sides.

Across a field of chest-high corn, a spooked crow began cawing from a maple tree.

A cop for 18 years, Sheriff's Detective Wendell Roddy had sifted for evidence in more garbage bins than he could remember. He had smelled worse, but that hardly made the task at hand any easier. He folded his glasses, slipped them into his right pants pocket, and then hoisted himself over the dumpster's side.

A bullet. A gun. A body even. Anything could be here. A purse. A blouse. Keys. Nothing could be here, too. Any scrap of paper could be an essential clue.

Or nothing but a scrap of paper.

Roddy picked through the garbage, crushing maggots and stirring up flies.

At the Kunzes' farm, bedlam.

The dirt road in front the house had become impassibly clogged with squad cars, vans from the State Crime Laboratory, the fat American sedans and pick-up trucks that belonged to neighbors, rescue workers and volunteer search patrol members and the skinny Japanese two-doors that belonged to the print, radio and television reporters, as well as their photographers, cameramen and producers.

Their wheels stirred up so much road dust that onlookers held moistened bandanas to their mouths, and the leaves of the trees around Kenny's trailer turned beige.

A quarter-mile north, in the Kunzes' garden, deputies snapped pictures of tire tracks, broken tomato plants and footprints.

Sheriff Schillinger felt confident that Helen's body, and perhaps even the murder weapon, were nearby, and he organized search crews to comb the farm's fields, sheds, woods and ditches. He gave up joining in the crews himself when a video crew stuck a camera in his face and backed its way down between the two rows of corn he was trying to look through.

"I'll be lucky if I can find my car in this mess," he said.

Eileen Moore tapped the side of the dumpster and Roddy looked up. She was wondering if it would be all right if maybe she and Don Schauer, her production supervisor, stopped by the Kunz house to see how Kenny was doing. Maybe bring him some food, if that was all right.

"Kenny's by his Aunt Germaine in Abbotsford," he said. "He'd probably be glad to see you."

A brown United Parcel Post truck picked its way through the gridlock surrounding the Kunzes' farm and stopped in the middle of the dirt road at the base of the Kunzes' driveway. The driver hopped down from the truck, a small brown paper package in one arm, a clipboard in the other.

"You're going to have to move the truck," a deputy told the driver.

"I've got a package here for Randy Kunz," the driver said.

Detective Hoenisch was called over and the package was handed to him. Hoenisch took the package to the crime lab truck and carefully opened the box.

It contained two video tapes: *Campus Fever* and *Campus Fever II*.

Roddy found nothing in the dumpster.

And he found nothing in Kenny's locker either, except an empty can of Pabst Blue Ribbon, a 1984 Milwaukee Brewers schedule and a dirty white bib. Eileen Moore invited him into her office for a cup of coffee.

"Cream with that?"

"No," Roddy said. He coughed a little to quiet his stomach. "No, but thank you."

Don Schauer came in, poured out a cup of coffee and sat down.

"Don has worked here longer than anyone, except Kenny," Eileen Moore said.

"I'd say I might know Kenny about as well as anyone around here, but that ain't saying much," Schauer said. Schauer was wearing a white paper cap. He took it off his head and folded it flat.

"You could never tell if he was happy or sad," Schauer said. "His face always looked the same. He never said much, and when he did, you couldn't understand a damn thing."

"The factory can be noisy," Moore said.

"Yep. So if and when he'd say something, you'd have to say, 'What? What's that?' about a dozen times. It seemed to go better if you didn't try to have much conversation with him."

Roddy jotted notes into his pad. He smiled and huffed at the appropriate moments.

"I read in the paper that them Kunzes was all shot with a .22," Schauer said.

"We was talking about that this morning—the other workers and me. Kenny had two .22-caliber weapons, you know."

Roddy looked up.

"Two?"

"Yeah. Helmut says—Helmut Bernt, who knows the family real well—Helmet says Kenny's got a .22 single-shot rifle and he's got a .22-caliber pistol."

"Beer?"

"No thanks."

Ken Fasse shrugged, then settled into an easy chair beside an opened window. Across his living room sat Detective Roddy, politely smiling.

"Unbelievable," Fasse said. He popped open a can of Pabst and sighed, forcing a little stream of air through the gap between his two front teeth.

"I'm 64 years old," Fasse said. "I've had four heart attacks. I've been Ken Kunz's friend for damn near 20 years. Never thought I'd live to see the day something like this . . ."

"You say you're pretty good friends with Kenny?" Roddy asked.

"Sure. Sure. Well, we take my camper and go fishing together. Been fishing three times this summer so far. Family's kind of—they were kind of—backward, you know. I've always sort of felt sorry for them."

Fasse looked out the window, sipped his beer and said, "I had this agreement with Kenny, see. I'd drive my tractor up there, with a wood splitter and all, and I'd help them split up firewood. In return, I could help myself to all the wood I wanted.

"Their place was a real mess. So I tried to help them with some of the necessities, like firewood. See, a long time ago I give Kenny a ride home from Kraft—I use to drive a truck there—and I see this old woman, who turned out to be Irene, out there with an axe, whacking away at some logs.

"Now Irene's no bigger than a young girl. She was strong, though. She sunk that axe into a big thick log, then couldn't yank it out. So she just lifted that axe, block of wood on it and all, and brought them down—Bam!"

Fasse sipped.

"Split it," he said.

"Still, it didn't seem right. They was so old. So I started going out there to help with the wood. Help with the garden."

"What about Randy?" Roddy asked.

"Oh, Randy. Randy never lifted a finger. Never did a thing. Randy never worked a day in his life. Kenny wasn't exactly an over-achiever either, you know. Last week I was up there helping Helen hill potatoes. Kenny was suppose to be helping, but he was nowhere. I had to go bang on his trailer door and tell him to get his ass in gear."

"Tell me about Helen," Roddy said.

"Gentle," Ken Fasse said.

"Like last week, when we was hilling potatoes. I shoved my spade into the ground and I'll be damned, overturned a nest of mice. Little blind baby things. I was going to mash them. They're pests, right? So I lifted my shovel and just then I looked over at Helen and she had her hand up and she had this look in her eyes—I don't know. It's her garden. So I left them alone.

"She went over and picked up the mice and patted them back into their nest. Like they was her children."

Ken Fasse looked out his window and sipped his beer.

"They was like children," he said. "Kunzes, I mean.

"Back in June, Helen was telling me that a man had come to their house looking for antiques. She tells me she just let the man into the house and the garage to look around. I says, 'Helen. You can't be doing that sort of thing. It's not safe.' She don't say nothing. Just looks at me.

"They were always being taken advantage of. They'd buy just about anything anyone tried to sell them. Couple of weeks ago I was in their garage and the old set of cupboards that was there was missing. I says to Helen, 'Where's the cupboards?'

"She don't say anything. You don't know if they're stolen or what."

─────── 2 ───────

From *The Milwaukee Sentinel*
July 7, 1987:

> The slaying of the Kunz family in the Town of Bern is the third multiple murder within a 15-mile radius of northwestern Marathon County in as many years.
>
> On Feb. 28, Edward Langbecker, 74, and his wife, Ruth, 68, were stabbed and beaten to death at their Town of Hamburg farmhouse. The town is less than 10 miles from the Town of Bern.
>
> Also in Hamburg, Peter Reinke, 42, his wife, Carolyn, 40, and their son, Timothy, 18, were found shot to death in their home April 7, 1984. The Reinkes' daughter, Christine, 12, was wounded in the incident.
>
> Investigators said they have no reason to believe there is any connection between the three cases.

At the northwest corner of the room that Helen and Randy had shared was a set of steps—you couldn't call them stairs, really—rickety steps that led to a rectangular hole in the ceiling. Climb through the hole, and you are Alice down the rabbit hole, a visitor to a world vaguely like the one you have left, only quite a bit more curiouser.

The attic was a single room, as large as the house and lighted by three small windows. Stifling hot in the summer. Frigid in the winter. Always dusty.

The Kunz family, it seemed, had never thrown a thing away, ever, and what was not stacked in piles throughout the downstairs was spread in layers throughout the attic.

Farming equipment and medicines for cattle, maternity clothes, clothing for babies, Kenny's black panda bear, missing one eye, a

Kewpie doll Helen had won tossing yellow rings onto a milk jug at a county fair, mattresses, pots and pans, old fur coats, boxes of canned foods, a pool table without its legs, a vibrating football field without its plastic players, a Monopoly game without its little green houses and red hotels.

Sheriff LeRoy Schillinger stood on the steps and wondered if the floor of the attic would hold his weight and wondered if beneath a box, or rolled up in a rug, or chopped into pieces and stuffed in some bags, was the body of Helen Kunz.

From *The Wausau Daily Herald*
July 10, 1987:

Attic Boxes Searched for Kunz

The Marathon County Sheriff's Department searched through 100 boxes and bags in the Kunz family farmhouse attic.

Investigators used a tractor with a scoop to lift boxes down from an attic window and over to a shed, where they inspected and stored the contents.

"We're looking for Helen," Schillinger said. "She certainly could be in one of those bags or boxes.

"That would be a good place to hide someone if you don't look."

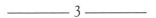

——— 3 ———

Schillinger was a tall man with an easy way about him and a reflexive smile. He looked something like a cross between Sheriff Andy Taylor and Fred Flintstone.

Schillinger dropped out of high school after his junior year and joined the Marshfield Police Department when he was 24. Five years later, he quit the department to open a gas station. Three years later, he became chief of the tiny Stratford Police Department, where he remained until he was elected sheriff in 1986.

He was touchy about not having a high school diploma.

"It's a piece of paper," he'd say. Does that make me great because I have a piece of paper? Does that piece of paper make me qualified?

"I don't think so," he'd say.

Diploma or not, it was clear that nothing had prepared Schillinger for a case as complex as the Kunz murders or for the frenzied onslaught of reporters it attracted.

During the first days of the investigation, his department spent 450 man-hours erecting roadblocks to keep the media away from the Kunz house, and it seemed as if every move he made—driving his car, eating his lunch, scratching his butt—was photographed or filmed.

In an effort to manage the press, he began to hold news conferences twice daily, allowing reporters to clip microphones to his tie and coat as he stood in front of the Marathon County Courthouse, responding as politely as possible to reporters, though they seemed to ask him the same questions over and over and over.

"Where's Helen?"

"I don't know," he said. "Basically, the investigation centers around that big mystery: Where is Helen Kunz? She's the key. If we can find her, then we can solve the mystery of what happened here."

"What's the motive? Any suspects?"

"We can't identify suspects," he said. "At this point, everybody is a suspect.

"The victims were killed in an assassination/execution style by someone who was definitely demented or who went wild. We figure the murders happened before 11 p.m. Helen and Randy went to see the fireworks in Athens and got home around 10:30 or a quarter to 11 p.m.

"It is possible they knew the victims.

"We don't believe burglary was the motive. They paid for everything in cash, but their income was small. The house was full of junk, with nothing of any real value in there."

"Is Helen a suspect?"

"If she doesn't turn up as a victim. She was a pretty small woman, but she was pretty spry, from what I hear."

"What's going on in the garden north of the house?"

"There are three sets of tire tracks on the small road leading to the garden. One belongs to a car owned by Randy Kunz, one of the victims. The other belongs to a car owned by Kenny Kunz, the survivor.

"There's a third set of tracks out there that we're not sure of yet. We're taking a close look at that."

From a Sheriff's Investigative report entitled "Neighborhood Canvass":

Detective Krueger: Let's see. You're Wilmer, and your wife is Evelyn?

Resident: Yeah.

Detective: Who lives here with you?

Resident: Just my wife and I.

Detective: Okay. Do you know anybody who lives around here or lives anywhere who might have occasion to drive past the residence there on Townline Road on a regular basis—like to and from work, or maybe has a relation?

Resident: Well, Bartkik's got a relation over there—Eugene Bartnik. He used to have heifers down there. I don't know if he does now or not. He use to go by there. And Howard Bedroski. He's got land right there.

Detective: Yeah. I think we've already talked to him.

Resident: You know a helicopter landed right on his oats!

Detective: Is that right? That's the TV camera people who do that. That isn't us.

Resident: Right in the oats.

From *The Wausau Daily Herald* editorial page,
July 15, 1987:

For more than a week now, the news media have filled
our eyes and our ears with stories of the Kunz murders.

What we know—the minutiae of their lives, their
secrets, their scandals—would be none of our business under different circumstances. But the murder
has left them open to the closest scrutiny. Their deaths
have made their lives a matter of public record.

That is as legitimate as it is unfortunate. Murder is
news. Neighbors are fearful. People have a right to
know if their fears are warranted.

If publicity—even about events long past—can help
apprehend the killer or killers, it is not only justified,
it is essential.

From *The Wausau Daily Herald* front page,
July 10, 1987:

Psychic Doubts Helen Kunz
Is Still Alive

An area psychic said she has received impressions
about the Kunz murder case and may know the
whereabouts of Helen Kunz, 70, missing since Saturday night.

Robin—who asks that her last name not be used—is
a Schofield woman who claims to have clairvoyant
powers. She says her help has been sought by police in
six states.

She has not been contacted by the Marathon County
authorities in regard to the Kunz case, but Thursday
night she talked about the case with the *Wausau
Daily Herald.*

"With Helen, the word 'corn' came into my head very strongly," she said.

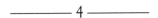

———— 4 ————

Pompous editorials and goofy news stories did little to endear the media to the people living in western Marathon County.

The sudden cavalcade of big-city journalists, television crews and photographers both terrified and embarrassed the community, xenophobic by nature, at a particularly critical and frightening juncture in its history.

Within days of the murders, a photocopied letter on ruled notebook paper began showing up in stores around Athens. Addressed to the media, it said:

"What difference does it make what kind of groceries the family purchased at the local grocery store or the bakery?

"And to dig up things that happened 50 years ago is getting pretty low. Everybody has a ghost or two in their closet.

"Think of the family that is left.

"How do you expect them to keep living after this?"

Sheriff Schillinger began bringing his own tape recorder to news conferences.

"There's a lot of rumors out there," he said.

"What we have under investigation I am not going to release unless it is something that the public really wants to know."

An irritant, perhaps, but it was the media that uncovered one of the most substantive leads early in the investigation. The story, filed on July 7 by Associated Press reporter Maryann Mrowca, sent the rest of the media scrambling to match it, and would change the Sheriff's Department's entire approach to Helen Kunz's disappearance:

Athens, Wis. -AP- Seventy-year-old Helen Kunz, who has been missing since the bodies of her brother, two sisters and son were found in their farmhouse near here Sunday, bought a box of .22-caliber ammunition at a hardware store recently, the store owner said.

Preliminary autopsy reports indicate that the victims had each been shot twice in the head with a .22-caliber pistol or rifle.

Helen Kunz bought a box of .22-caliber shells at Weiler's Hardware Store about four weeks ago, owner Dave Weiler said in an interview. He called her a regular customer, and said she seemed her normal sweet self during the purchase.

"She was a sweet little grandma. She wasn't a grandma, but she was that type," Weiler said.

Later, Gail Weiler would tell reporters that Helen had told her husband that the shells were for Randy to use for shooting birds.

"A lot of people were shooting blackbirds around then," she said.

But as Helen talked, Gail Weiler said, she grew upset.

"She told Dave she didn't like it that they were watching porno movies all the time on the VCR."

Helen said it made her so angry "I could kill them all," Weiler said.

"The only reason I remember it was she was so mad I thought, 'Whoa. She didn't really like that,'" she said.

When reporters asked Schillinger about the Associated Press story, he looked shocked and said he was unaware of the purchase.

"If it happened, I don't think it's trivial," he said.

From *The Milwaukee Sentinel*,
July 9, 1987:

Sheriff LeRoy Schillinger backed away from earlier statements in which he said Kunz was somewhere on the 108-acre Town of Bern farm.

He would not elaborate on the new direction of the search, except to say the woman's description had "been put out nationwide."

The bodies of Irene, Marie, Clarence and Randy were cremated, sparing Kenny and his Aunt Germaine the spectacle of four caskets crammed into the tiny parlors of the Kramer Funeral Home in Athens.

The ashes were placed in small canisters, and while a half-dozen reporters sat on the steps of the Athens Community Hall across the street, about 20 people gathered at the funeral home for a private service.

It was hot and humid, and mourners entered the funeral home frightened and uncomfortable. A video camera hidden in the lobby by the Sheriff's Department recorded them mopping their foreheads with hankies, tightening their ties, tugging down their slips, glancing around.

Immediate family members had arrived an hour early, escorted by deputies through a back door. They were greeted by Tom Kraemer and Father Len Stashek, a priest at St. Thomas Catholic Church, where Anna Kunz had been a member for years.

When it came time for the service, Stashek stood up and said a few words.

"It is very difficult to express our sympathy to Germaine and Kenneth because of the circumstances, the curiosity, questions and sense of loss," he said.

"Our consolation is what they think is right for them. The Kunzes were probably not very comfortable with society, but they were comfortable with their lives."

Kenny shifted in his seat.

He hadn't attended church too often, but he maintained a simple and deep belief in God. He couldn't hear what the priest was saying very well, but he believed he was being comforted.

From a Marathon County Sheriff's Department report, filed by Detective Rick Schroeder:

> During the time of the service, I maintained a surveillance of the area outside the funeral home, at which time I copied plate numbers of any vehicles in the immediate area. I observed several news people in the area.

After the services, I again contacted Tom Kraemer and Father Stashek in reference to anything they observed of the participants in the memorial service. They stated no one appeared to act out of the ordinary and appeared to be reacting natural to the circumstances.

Kenny followed Germaine out a back door, taking off his sport coat before climbing into her car. He rolled down his window and waited for Germaine to settle into the passenger's seat. She started the car, but then just sat there, weeping into a tissue. With the scarf tied around her head, Kenny thought she looked like his mother.

The remains were to be buried later, once Helen was found. Kenny drove through Athens, past the bank, past Weiler's Hardware Hank, past Hartman's Variety, past the little white pavilion in the village square, past the IGA Food Store. They turned left, and after a few hundred yards, they were outside the village limits.

They passed a sign that said, "A family that prays together, stays together." Then the road turned to dust.

Chapter 2

How Intricate
the Dust

——— 1 ———

From *The Wausau Daily Herald*, top of the front page, July 11, 1987:

NOTHING NEW IN KUNZ CASE

On Saturday, July 11, a fierce storm blew across Wisconsin.

Clouds churned and climbed into piles. Winds gusted to near 80 mph. Hail mixed with rain and fell with such force that people pulled their cars onto the shoulder of the interstate leading into Marathon County. There they waited out the storm, wipers wiping back and forth and headlights shining into the midday dark.

An unmarked squad car, driven by Detective Roddy, swooshed past them. Beside him sat Kenny Kunz. In the back seat, Detective Hoenisch.

"Quite a storm," Roddy said. Hoenisch nodded.

"We could use a little rain, couldn't we, Ken," Hoenisch said.

The two detectives were taking Kenny to his aunt's house. Kenny had spent most of the afternoon taking a lie detector test at the Sheriff's headquarters in Wausau.

Kenny had done quite poorly.

The three men sat around Germaine's kitchen table. Germaine had fixed them each a cup of coffee before she was shuttled off to a daughter's house. Outside, in an unmarked car, two deputies kept watch, jotting down the license plate numbers of cars they considered suspicious.

Hoenisch placed a tape recorder in the center of the table and began to read Kenny his rights.

"Okay, Ken. I need you to—I would like you to sign right here by the 'X.' That means we went over all that and that you understand each of these rights. Okay?"

"What's the question again?"

"Do you understand these rights?"

"Yeah."

"Okay. Now read along here—'Realizing that you have these rights, are you now willing to talk to us and answer our questions?'"

"Well," Kenny said. "Some."

He took the pen from Hoenisch's hand and signed. His hands shook as he signed. Hoenisch reached out to take back his pen, but Kenny's hand shook so violently that Kenny could only place the pen on the table then thrust his hands into the pockets of his coat.

"Germaine don't like this," Kenny said.

"Well, you seem sort of upset right now, Ken. Are you?"

The wind pushed against the house.

"Little upset. Too much."

"Too much what?"

"Too much excitement."

"Too much excitement?"

"Too much."

Roddy removed his glasses, placed them on the table, and closed his note pad.

"We're not going to hurt you in any way, Ken. We're not going to hurt you in any way. We're your friends. All we want to do is figure out what happened at your home. Do you understand that?"

"I know."

Roddy spoke very softly.

"We're not going to get after you. You're not in custody. You understand that? We haven't arrested you for anything, have we? All we want to do is talk about the polygraph, the lie detector operator. For some reason, you reacted strongly to his questions. Now maybe the questions were phrased the wrong way."

Roddy paused. Kenny, who had been looking down, looked up at him.

"Maybe it would be possible you had nothing to do with it, but have some knowledge of what happened. You know what I mean? Maybe that is why the machine—or you—reacted. Maybe you weren't even there. Know what I mean?"

Kenny sighed.

"So would it be possible you reacted to those questions because did Helen ever talk to you about being mad about those dirty movies? And did she ever talk to you about buying bullets or something to do with a gun? Maybe you had no part in it, Ken, but maybe you know what happened. Maybe that's why the machine reacted the way it did."

"I didn't know about the bullets," Kenny said. "Not till it was on TV."

"See what Wendell is saying?" Hoenisch said. He felt nervous and tongue-tied.

"Maybe over the last two, three months, for example, talking about the dirty movies. You've only had the VCR since December, right? And you gave Helen and Randy the money to buy that—but maybe since Randy started watching the movies and apparently some of the other people in the house, maybe Helen's been upset about that.

"Maybe she didn't like that, and it's possible she told you she didn't like that and that it bothered her a lot, and she should do something to take care of the problem.

"Do you understand what I'm saying? Maybe she told you many times how much it bothered her and maybe she told you many times what she thought she should do about it, and now something's happened. Maybe in the back of your mind you're saying, 'Well, I was

101

at Kraft all night—which might have been—but I think I know what happened here and why it happened.' "

Hoenisch looked at Kenny and paused. Kenny had pushed away from the table a little and had tucked his chin down into his chest.

"You understand what I'm saying?"

Kenny didn't look up.

"Yeah."

Hoenisch pressed on.

"I think, for example, when you get up to the house—if I were in your shoes, and that had happened, if I had heard my mother complaining for months about what's going on at the house and how she planned on taking care of the problem, and I come home and see something like that—my first thought would be, 'Well, Mom must have done something to take care of the problem.'

"But you don't want anyone else to know that, which is probably a natural reaction. Everybody is going to want to protect their mother. That's what I was trying to get at before. Maybe the results of the tests were because deep down inside, you have some thoughts as to what happened, but you just don't want to tell anybody, but you can't control what the machine picks up and that's why it reads the way it does.

"You can sit here and tell Wendell and me that you didn't fire the gun, that you were at Kraft all night, you didn't do it. But deep down inside, while you're telling us that, you might be thinking, 'Helen had to do it. She was the only one that could have done it and she complained about what was going on at the house. I figured she was going to do something 'cause she was mad at what they were doing at the house.' "

Roddy and Hoenisch stared at Kenny. They could hear the clock on the stove tick and the rain drum against the roof.

"You can tell us and tell anybody anything you want," Hoenisch said. "But deep down inside, you've got in your own mind, you've got to be thinking about what happened up there. That's the kind of stuff we want to talk to you about. Like I told you the other day, you're the only one who knows what's been going on up there. Do you understand what we're saying, Ken?"

Roddy cleared his throat and said, "Ken, did she ever talk to you about any problems she had? Or did she talk to Randy more than you? If something was bothering her."

The two men waited. Finally, Kenny said, "Well, she never said nothing that something was bothering her."

"Did she ever talk to you about how she disliked those movies that showed too much on the screen?" Roddy asked.

"She never told me much about it. We really didn't have— sometimes we had "R," but there wasn't very much on there. There were never no "X" movies."

"Were you aware of any movies that they bought through the mail that were sent there that were "X" rated?" Roddy asked.

"No. I never did. Didn't know they had movies."

"Why would they buy dirty movies and not let you see them?"

"I don't know. I never knew they had any. They don't tell me."

"You had some pretty dirty magazines in your trailer, didn't you?" Roddy said.

Kenny turned crimson.

"Those are my magazines," he said.

"There were dirty magazines in the house. Helen, this bothered her so much, she talked to people in town. We have people that she talked to that she complained about the dirty movies and even made the comment that she 'could kill them all.'"

"Helen did?" Kenny asked.

"Yes. And I find it hard to believe that she could have done this on her own. Who would she confide in or who would she talk to to help her do this job?"

"You got me there too, also."

"You know you're the only one who can help us, Ken, get to the bottom of this. We want to get to the bottom of this as much as you do."

Kenny nodded. His frown deepened.

"I don't think there would be too many people here who'd want to—there wouldn't be—I can think of nobody around that area that would do it for her, if she would really want somebody to do it for her."

The cassette tape reached the end of one side, and as Hoenisch flipped it over, Roddy got up to stretch his legs. He wandered over to the living room window and watched the rain pour down. A birch branch tumbled past, driven by the wind.

He decided that when they resumed, he would let go of the lie detector angle and take another tack.

"Going back to last Saturday, Ken," he said. "You worked from 9:00 in the morning until, what was it—5:00 or 5:30?"

"5:30."

"Now your lunch hour. I think you told us before, Ken, that your mom fixed your lunch. How long of a lunch did you get?"

"Half an hour."

"Did you eat lunch at the plant, or did you leave at noon? Did you go any place at noon in your car? Did you go for a ride or anything?"

"I might have . . ."

"Where? Where would you have gone?"

"I go up to the garden. I wouldn't have gone home."

"Okay. Well, apparently you did Saturday, because we had somebody that saw you go by. You had a white hat on, you had your working clothes on, so it's a possibility that you did go up to the garden."

Kenny nodded.

"Okay. So then you got off work. You worked the rest of the afternoon and you got off work at 5:30, right?

"5:30."

"Where is it you went first then?"

"Over to Wally's bar."

"Wally's. And how many beers was it you said you had at Wally's bar?"

"Well, I'd say half a dozen glasses."

"Okay. So then do you have any idea what time it was when you left Wally's?"

"Ten after seven."

"Where did you go from there?"

"Home."

"You went home. And what did you do at home?"

"First I changed clothes."

"You took your whites off. Okay."

"Went in the house."

"Okay."

"Stayed home until about 8:00. I talked to Helen and Randy."

"What were they doing?"

"Sitting on the bed over where the VCR was. They had the radio on. They didn't have no TV on."

"Okay."

"Talking about going to—asked them about going to the fireworks. They says they think they're going, but wasn't sure. I talked about the garden then . . ."

"You talked about the garden?"

"I says, 'I'm going up to my garden,' and I don't know. We talked about something and I forgot. Anyway, everything was normal."

"Nobody seemed mad. Helen and everybody?"

"Not that I noticed any difference there."

"So then what did you do, Ken?"

"At 8:00 I went up there. The garden. I drive up there on the road, then I walk in."

"Okay."

"I backed out again when I went home. It was about 10:00. It's dark. It was dark already."

"You said you had rototilled. What was it you rototilled that night?"

"Some cabbage and beans. Peas."

"Did you have any beer at home or in the garden?"

"Two cans up in the garden. And I had some in the car."

"So you left about 10:00. Where did you go?"

"I wanted to go by Jerkwater tavern, but it was closed. So I went down to Milan. Parked down at the factory and drove the car inside and locked the doors. Nobody else could get in."

"Then?"

"Not too much. Kind of sat around."

"Drink some more beer?"

"I had a few. Three for sure. Just was celebrating a little bit."

"You were just celebrating a little bit."

"I wasn't drunk or nothing. Then I just fell asleep."

"Do you remember what time you woke up?"

"Well, I didn't sleep all the while, but it was about 4:00 I guess. I know I left about 20 minutes after 4:00 from the factory."

"Do you remember stopping anywhere before you went to Kraft?"

"I didn't stop no place."

Roddy pulled a slip of paper from his shirt pocket. It was a copy of a receipt from Milan Co-op gas pump. It showed Kenny had gotten gas for his car that night a few minutes before 10 p.m.

"See. It prints the time. It tells us what time you were there. And it was around 10:00. In fact, we have somebody that saw you when you where there."

Hoenisch spoke: "Ken. Do you remember yesterday when we were coming to Wausau for the blood and stuff and I asked you when was the last time you got gas? 'First part of the week.' Remember that?"

"Only thing we're getting at," said Roddy, "is that wouldn't it be possible that maybe you had more to drink than you thought? Would you have had that much to drink that you don't even know you bought gas?"

Kenny shook his head. He picked up the slip of paper. "I was thinking—Oh. I said . . ."

"And what we're concerned about, Ken, is this: We got a witness that saw you driving north from Milan toward your home before 11:00, but after 10:30 at night."

Kenny shook his head. He looked at the two detectives, then shook it again.

"I stayed at the factory."

"You're sure you stayed at the factory?"

"That's right. I didn't keep no track of when I got gas. I didn't mark it down."

"Well, that's probably true," Hoenisch said. "And I'd be hard pressed to remember that last time I got gas. But the point is, you seem to remember everything else pretty good, Ken, what you did Saturday night. At least what you think you did.

"You have to look at our position. Ken says he doesn't remember going up to the garden Saturday afternoon. Somebody sees him. Now he does. Ken says he doesn't remember getting gas, but somebody sees him. Now he does. Ken doesn't remember driving toward his house at 11 . . ."

"I'm sure I wasn't," Kenny said. "I stayed at the factory. I didn't go. Didn't leave there."

There was silence. Then Roddy said, "We tend to believe you, Ken.

"But all we are saying is that maybe you had too much to drink and can't remember going some place. This test. Why did the test show such a large reaction to your answers? Is there something you know, Ken? Is there something you know? Maybe you had no part of it. But is there something you know that you're afraid to tell us? Because right now, we want to help you. We want to help Helen. Can you give us some idea where we can find her? Where can we find Helen?"

"Wasn't nowhere that night. I wouldn't know what happened. No."

Hoenisch sighed. Roddy stood up and opened the refrigerator and peered inside.

"It's—you almost have to believe she had something to do with it," he said. He closed the door.

"She said 'I should kill them all. She bought .22 shells. All four were killed with .22 shells. And the fourth fact is, everybody else that lived in the house is dead. Except her. She's not there."

Roddy sat down at the table and waited for Kenny to look at him. When he did, he said, "'I should kill them all.' Wouldn't you kind of believe she meant it?"

"Well, yeah," Kenny said. "You got something there. But I told you what I walked into that morning. I didn't expect to see that. I don't know what to say."

"We don't want the news to get ahold of this. It's just between us. But I just want to make you understand why it's obvious to us that Helen is somewhat involved."

"I don't know where she went to," Kenny said. "Don't know."

The tape stopped. Hoenisch ejected it, inserted a fresh cassette. Kenny asked if he could go to the bathroom. When he came back to

107

the table, he stood behind his chair a few moments before sitting down.

"Right now, it's a toss-up," Hoenisch said. "It's your word against the other person's. Someone saw you going up toward your house about 11 that night. You say you were at Kraft."

"You putting the blame on me?"

"We're not putting the blame on you, but we certainly have to look at you and take everything into consideration with what we have. You can come up with all sorts of theories. We came up with a theory that maybe at 7:30 you went up and worked the garden, and after Helen and Randy go to the fireworks, you go down to the house and Clarence is apparently sleeping, Irene is apparently sleeping, Marie is by the door . . ."

"I didn't."

"This is just a theory. I'm not saying you did this now. But say if you did, if you were involved in somehow in what happened to Clarence, Irene and Marie at the house—you go down to Milan to get some gas and the fireworks are supposed to end around 11:00, so you go home and park your car by the garden. And you walk back down to the house and you wait for Randy to come and you go out and you hop into Randy's car and you drive it back up to the garden, hop into your own car and Randy's car stays there. It fits, doesn't it?"

"I wasn't . . ."

Roddy stopped him.

"We have someone else, Ken, who said they know you had a gun about a year ago—a .22 pistol."

"A year ago?"

"They said they saw it about a year ago and they asked even to buy it from you and you didn't want to sell it," Roddy said.

"I didn't have no gun."

"Now we have a test—a paraffin test—that we can put some chemical on your hands and then we can tell if you shot a gun within the last two weeks." Roddy glanced at Hoenisch. There was no such test, and he wanted the younger detective to follow his bluff. Hoenisch's expression remained absolutely unaltered.

"You can wash your hands all you want, Ken, and it won't come off. You would be willing to take this test, wouldn't you. Would you let us put that on your hands and see if there was any gun powder on there?"

"There's no gun powder on there," Kenny said. "I didn't have no gun."

"So there'd be no reason why you wouldn't want to take that test—let us put that powder on your hands, that chemical, and see if it turns color?"

"No," Kenny said. "I know you don't believe me, what I say. But it's true. I wouldn't shoot nobody."

"Ken," Hoenisch said. "We have to look at the evidence we have."

"You have the wrong person, though. Wasn't me and I didn't do it."

"Throughout the years, Ken, we've had a lot of people say that. People who really did do it."

"I know. I imagine. But why would I do it, you know. Why?"

"One thing I can think of real fast," Roddy said, "is that you had too much to drink and didn't know what you were doing. Who knows? You black out and do something—let's say you go home, whatever happens, happens, you get rid of the gun and you go back to the plant. Then you wake up and don't remember doing anything."

"I didn't do it."

"You know what another theory is that I had since?" Hoenisch said. "That you didn't do it—that you had nothing to do with it until you got home and you saw what happened. Somewhere in the house or by the house is Helen with the gun. Helen's dead. Helen committed suicide. And this has happened before, where someone will change a scene because they don't want people to know that their mother or brother or whoever committed suicide. Again, it's just a theory. You come home and see what's there—you find Helen with a gun—and for some reason you take Helen and the gun wherever so she can't be found. That way people won't know Helen shot these people and killed herself.

"Do you understand that, Ken? Is it possible that that happened? Do you understand that?"

"I get the idea of it," Kenny said. "You're worrying something in between that's bothering."

"Ah, sure," Hoenisch said. He exchanged glances with Roddy. "Is that what happened, Ken?"

"Afraid not, no. No, it didn't."

This time when the tape reached its end, all three men remained in their chairs. Kenny asked if he could get a glass of water, and Hoenisch said "Take mine," and slid his cup across the the table.

When the tape restarted, Roddy decided to shake things up. He asked, "Who's your dad?"

"I don't know."

"Didn't you tell one of the officers that Clarence—you thought Clarence was your dad?"

"I said maybe, but I don't know." Kenny wrapped his arms across his chest.

"Over the years, have you seen Clarence—have you ever known them to have sex?"

"I'm not saying."

"So apparently there's some truth to it. What bothers me—what really bothers me, Ken, is that when I asked you about those "X" rated movies that were all over the house, I can't believe that you never seen any. You never had a girlfriend? Have you ever had sex?"

"Afraid not."

"Pardon me?"

"No."

"You never had sex with a woman? Have you ever had sex with Helen?"

"No."

"Who was the father of Randy?"

"I don't know."

"Do you have any idea?"

"I don't know."

"Could Clarence be the father of Randy?"

"I don't know."

"Could you be the father of Randy?"

"No. I never touched Helen."

"Do you think Randy did? Do you think Randy had sex with Helen?"

"I don't know."

"Randy and Helen slept in the same bed, is that true?"

"Yeah."

"Could it be that you and Randy are watching these dirty movies and getting all sexed up and getting horny and after Helen and that's why Helen got mad?"

"I never got after Helen. I didn't know they had those movies in there."

"Well that's the part I find hard to believe, that makes me feel you're not being truthful with us. Those movies were all over the place. Ken, they were laying out. You could see them. They're in boxes with pictures of girls on them. Every time you walked into that room."

"I didn't know they had them."

"Ken, we're not trying to pry into your personal lives. But I think it's important that you tell us what you know about the sexual affairs that went on in that house."

"Well, it's going to stay here, though."

"It's going to stay here."

Kenny drank Hoenisch's water. The detective went to the sink and refilled the glass.

"Well, I know that years ago Clarence was—Clarence and Helen. I don't know what to say."

"How many years ago?"

"I was milking cows yet. It could have been about 10 years ago."

"So they were having sex up to about ten years ago that you know of?"

Kenny sat in silence for more than a moment. He lifted his hands to his forehead and left them there, a curtain between himself and the world, a shield protecting him.

"I don't know what to say." The words were muttered like a moan.

"Pardon me?" Roddy kept his voice firm. Hard.

"I know when they were young they used to. I don't know how long after that."

"Okay. Did Clarence have sex with the other girls?"

"I don't think so."

"Not that you know of?"

"Helen. I know Helen—Helen was the one . . ."

"Helen was the only one that you seen him have sex with?"

Kenny placed his head against his shoulder and closed his eyes. "Awful young yet."

"How old were you when you last saw that, Ken?"

"This was—I was young."

"Well, would they have sex right in front of you? Where would they have sex?"

"Well, one night, I was along, and they—I was maybe 7 or 8 years old—they stopped on the road, town of Milan someplace, and they went in the back-seat of the old Model A Ford. Used to go there a few times."

"They did that a few times that you were along, and you remember that when you were young?"

"I imagine—they milked the cows together out there and probably did."

"You never caught them out there?"

"Not out there."

"That was before Randy was born. So it's a possibility that that's where Randy come from, is that right?"

"Possible."

"Don't you think, Ken, that if Randy was watching those kind of movies—do you think it's possible he started getting fresh with Helen?

"It's possible. Anything could be possible."

"That's his only companion, wasn't it?"

Hoenisch had been quiet for a while, jotting down notes. It was his turn.

"He's only 30 years old, Ken. It's human nature. It's not that he really was doing something wrong. I mean—it's only human nature. It's an animal instinct and drive and it's part of being a person. And he stayed home and the only person he did anything with was Helen.

So if he's going to go that direction any way at all, the only person to go towards is Helen. He didn't have any girlfriends. He didn't know any other—he wasn't in your situation when down at the plant you've got all the girls to at least intermingle with. He didn't have anybody else. So, he's grown up with Helen. I know you probably don't want to talk about it. You don't want to admit it. It's a very personal thing. We understand that. But if we're going to do a good job here, we've got to know everything."

It was a long speech, with no question to it. The three sat in silence. Something distant fell down in the wind.

"Do you have any suspicions of your own?" Hoenisch asked.

"Not really. They go to basketball games and baseball games. I don't know what's happening. They shared that bed together, but what's going on, I'm not there."

"You said a lot of times at night, you'd go watch a movie or something on TV."

"And they'd be—Randy and Helen—would be on the bed. When I got done, then I'd go out in the trailer and fall asleep and stay there until morning."

It was now a few minutes after 9 p.m. Roddy and Hoenisch had been questioning Kenny for about two hours and Kenny appeared pretty shaken. He dug a tissue out of his pants pocket and rubbed his eyes with it. He rubbed the thinning hair at the top of his head till it stood up like wheat stubble. He slouched into his chair so deeply that his chin rested on his chest.

As Hoenisch inserted a fresh tape, Roddy began:

"It's strange. You can understand our problem, can't you. All we know is that the movies are what made Helen angry. Okay? I don't think there would be any odds, it's so highly coincidental that Helen would buy bullets and make a statement that she should kill them all, and then three weeks later, everybody is found dead.

"It would be kind of unbelievable that Helen would make that statement, buy bullets—why would she buy bullets if she didn't have a gun? Right? Or have somebody that has a gun that told her to buy bullets. And then three weeks later, it would be awful coincidental if somebody come to rob them and then shot them all. But if somebody even come to rob them, why would they shoot everybody?"

Kenny didn't respond.

"Want something to drink, Ken?" Hoenisch asked.

Kenny shook his head.

"Nothing?"

Kenny gave no response.

"Ken. Like I said, this is between Wendell, you and me. You're the only person remaining right now that we can talk to. You're the only person that can tell us what went on in that house. Right now, sex seems to play a big part in what went on in the that house. You're 55 years old, Ken. There's no way I can believe that you can sit there and tell me that you've never had sex with a girl."

"They don't interest me."

"Some point in your life you had."

"Not home."

"I'm not saying at home. It could be Milan. Athens. It could be Wausau. It could be with a prostitute. I could be anywhere with anybody. I'm not saying at home. I'm not saying that, Ken."

"I didn't touch nobody at home."

"You had sex with a girl though, haven't you?"

"Not at the factory. None of those girls."

"It doesn't matter where, Ken. Okay? We're not trying to pin you down for sex with somebody somewhere."

"Not interested. No."

"Well, even if you weren't interested, I'd be willing to bet you still had sex with a girl."

Kenny looked at Hoenisch. "Think so?"

"Ha?" Hoenisch said. "At least once."

"It's possible," Kenny said. Quietly.

"Yes?"

"With a girl?" Kenny asked.

His tone was so quiet, Hoenisch could hardly hear him.

"You had sex with a girl?" Hoenisch asked.

"No."

"How about an animal," Roddy said. "Have you ever had sex with an animal?"

"No."

"That does happen," Roddy said. "That does happen."

"Might happen once," Kenny said. "Might have."

"You tried it."

"No," Kenny said. Then he muttered something. Hoenisch thought the conversation was getting a little too weird.

"Look, Ken. I can't believe you haven't had sex with a girl and I'll tell you why: all those books in your trailer. You're telling me you had no interest in girls, but if you're going to have all those books in your trailer with naked girls, then you have to have an interest. You had to have had sex with a girl."

"A little," Kenny said. "Messed around."

"And there's nothing wrong with that," Hoenisch said. "Like I said, that's human nature."

"Well, maybe I did. But I'd have to think of who."

"That's okay. You don't have to tell us who."

"Well, I'll say no more about that. It was nobody home."

"Okay," Hoenisch said. "Ken. Listen. Do you trust us, Wendell and me?"

"No."

"If I tell you that we're going to keep something secret, do you trust us?"

"No."

"Is there somebody else you'd rather talk to?"

"No. You can hear the secrets. I'm telling you what I think about. What I know. Don't know more about it."

"You can't believe, Ken, how something very small—something you don't think is important, can turn a whole case around. We have to have all that information so Wendell and I can sort through it and decide what's important and what's not important. Without it, it makes it that much harder for us to do our job. Pretty much as plain and simple as that. Now all you have to do is say yes or no. Okay?"

Kenny nodded.

"Have you ever had sex with a girl. Any girl. Yes or no."

"When I was younger. Nothing wrong with that. But I say, I never touched no one at home. Not even Helen. I know Clarence did. Clarence never had a girlfriend."

"Okay. Now about those videotapes. Let's say we fingerprint them. We're going to find Randy's fingerprints. We're going to find Helen's. You think your fingerprints are going to show up on any of those?

"I didn't know they was there, or I probably would have been watching them. Honest I didn't."

Kenny raised his voice slightly. It was two clicks above a whisper, but it was the loudest Roddy and Hoenisch had heard him speak. He looked at them and said: "You think I done it. But I didn't and I wouldn't have."

Hoenisch said: "I can't see inside you. I can't read your mind, so I don't know if you did it or not. All I can look at right now is what happened when you took that lie detector test. And for some reason, that machine indicated that you weren't being completely truthful with some of your answers. Don't ask me why. I don't know why. It bothers me that it turned out like that. And like I say, you're the only person that can sit there and know for sure that Kenny Kunz did not kill these people."

"What reason would I have?"

"Could you think of any?"

"I don't know. I don't know," Kenny said.

"Remember about three, four years ago in Hamburg that one young boy killed his mother and father? Reinke family. Remember that?"

"I probably heard about it."

"It was three, four years ago. Young boy killed his mother and father, brother, shot his little sister. There was no reason. He had no reason. He was 15 years old. Now what reason would a 15-year-old have to kill his whole family? There wasn't any problems there. Wasn't on drugs. Something happened. For some reason he did that, and that was that.

"Those things happen, Ken. They do. It happened. A person doesn't necessarily need a reason. Some people have a reason—a guy

Ignatz Kunz.

Anna Kunz.

Helen Kunz chases Randy during a celebration in Athens.

Ignatz Kunz holds Kenny outside
Kunzes' first farm, purchased in 1914
from the Rietbrock Land & Lumber Co.

Irene Kunz.

Marie Kunz.

Kenny Kunz, as a boy, outside the Kunzes' first farm.

Clarence and Ignatz.

Randy Kunz during his
senior year of high school.

Clarence Kunz.

Helen and Randy.

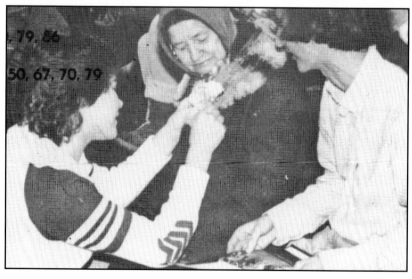

Helen and Randy as they receive a special award from the Athens High School Pep Club for their support of the school's athletic program. This is the picture that appeared in the school's 1984 yearbook. The picture appeared on an index page, and the numerals are page numbers.

Ken Fasse and Kenny Kunz during the summer of 1987.

Law enforcement officers search the Kunzes' farm.

Two Marathon County Sheriff's
investigators walk past Kenny's trailer
after leaving the Kunzes' home.

Marathon County Sheriff's
Detective Randall Hoenisch.

Marathon County Sheriff's
Detective Wendell Roddy.

Marathon County District
Attorney Rand Krueger.

Marathon County Sheriff
LeRoy Schillinger.

Milwaukee Sentinel

Detective Hoenisch pokes around with a shovel while investigators dig up a manure pit looking for Helen Kunz's remains.

Wausau Daily Herald

Sheriff Schillinger holds a news conference to announce that authorities have discovered remains they believe belong to Helen Kunz.

Chris Jacobs III walks with his mother, Judy, his father, Chris Jr., and his grandmother, Mary Prokopinski, behind their Town of Bern home.

Chris Jacobs appears in court with his attorney, Weldon Nelson, after being charged with obstructing a police search of his family's Marathon County farm.

Chris Jacobs, charged with five counts of being party to the crime of first-degree murder, watches as jury selection gets underway.

Milwaukee Journal

Kenny Kunz watches the
trial from a bench near the
back of the courtroom.

Milwaukee Journal

Judy Jacobs, seated behind
her son, watches the trial.

Marathon County Circuit Judge Vincent K. Howard.

Rand Krueger, acting as special prosecutor, carries an imprint of the tire recovered from Chris Jacobs.

Wausau Daily Herald

Chris Jacobs Jr. and friends react as the verdict is read.

Wausau Daily Herald

Chris Jacobs III smiles as he leaves the Marathon County Courthouse after being acquitted on all five counts.

Wausau Daily Herald

Kenny Kunz visits his family's grave.

goes to rob somebody; he's afraid he might be identified, and he'd maybe kill a person for that reason. A guy—a guy walks in his house and catches his wife in bed with another guy. He kills him. He's got a reason.

"But sometimes something happens and a person doesn't need a reason and it happens."

"I didn't have no reason."

"You don't have to. You don't have to have a reason."

"I never even thought about doing something," Kenny said. "Didn't have nothing planned."

"Well, neither did that kid in Hamburg, Ken. He didn't plan it. As far as we know, he had never thought about it before either. But something snapped. Like I say, you got a blackout—that's what scares me here—and it happens.

"The easiest thing would be if we knew you did it. Then we could work back and probably tell you why. If you told us right now, 'Yeah. I did it, but I don't know why I did it. I really don't remember much about it,' we could go from there and probably come up with a reason. Or maybe there is no reason. But there is no way we can sit here and guess at why you might want to do that."

Kenny shook his head.

"Well," Roddy said. "I bet Germaine's going to want to get back into her house. I think it's about time for Randy and me to go."

Kenny nodded and the two detectives stood up.

"What we talked about tonight—that's just between us three," Roddy said. "Okay? We don't want all that to get out to anybody. Okay?"

"No. I won't say."

"Okay," Roddy said. "That's nobody's business."

"The newspapers and on TV and all that," Hoenisch said.

"Yeah. If the newspapers or something try to talk to you, don't tell them anything."

Hoenisch picked up his tape recorder and flipped it off.

Chapter 3

Where's Helen?

From *The Wausau Daily Herald*, top of the front page
July 12, 1987

WHERE'S HELEN KUNZ?

Toward the end of the first week of the investigation, Sheriff Schillinger arrived at one of the daily 4 p.m. news briefings with a stack of photographs of Helen, which he distributed to all the reporters, along with a description:

"White female, 70 years of age. Approximately five feet tall, weighing 115 to 120 lbs. Blue-grey eyes. Hair brown, straight, parted down the middle. Cut at about half way down her neck. Arthritic. Swollen fingers and knuckles. Missing most of her teeth."

"Armed and dangerous?" a reporter asked.

Schillinger shot him a withering glance, but when he saw that the reporter was serious, he said, "We have not ruled out anything."

It wasn't a very good picture that Schillinger distributed to the media.

In 1984, the Athens High School Pep Club had presented Helen and Randy with a special award for their support of the school's athletic program. Even though Randy had graduated from the school nearly a decade earlier, he and Helen attended virtually every home baseball, basketball and football game they could. The two would come early to the games, sit away from the rest of the crowd, and even when it was stifling hot, Helen never removed her heavy black coat and the scarf she wore as a babushka.

The school's 1984 yearbook, "Athenian," carried a 2-by-3 inch snapshot of a cheerleader pinning a flower to the fur lapel of Helen's coat during an awards ceremony. Randy is seated beside her, holding what appears to be some kind of certificate. His hair hangs in his face. He is smiling. Around them is a blur of hands clapping.

Even in the photograph's original form, it is difficult to discern Helen's features. The top of her head is clipped off by the upper margin of the picture, and her face, what is visible of it from beneath her babushka, inclines sharply toward the flower.

But then reproduced in the yearbook, then copied and reproduced by the sheriff's department, then copied and reproduced by the wire service, then cropped tightly, enlarged and reproduced by the newspapers, the image becomes almost an abstraction. Details in the image are lost to each generation, until all that is left is the vague shadow of a nose, the suggestion of eyes, a blur of mouth.

This reductive Helen, reproduced almost daily in the papers, transmitted over news wires, faxed to police station's nationwide, photocopied and tacked to supermarket bulletin boards, beamed by microwave from television station to television station, accumulated almost iconic heft.

Over their morning cups of coffee, people glanced at the picture and filled in the details. And so, with time, Helen became an extension of them.

To them, her mystery became personal, keen.

From various reports filed with the Marathon County Sheriff's Department:

Mr. H. got off work at Hub City Jobbing, Marshfield, and went to the Central City Credit Union.

As he was leaving, he noticed a woman, quite elderly, walk out in front of his vehicle. This lady attempted to wave him down. In fact, he did stop and speak to her one minute.

Since this incident, he has seen the picture of Helen in the newspaper.

This incident reminded him of that woman.

The woman's description was: in her 70s, old and wrinkled. Small person. Deep voice. Real plain looking. Looked real poor and had a roundish face. Real gray hair.

She was carrying something, but he couldn't remember what it was. She asked him if he "was going north." She wanted a ride, he said.

He did not give her a ride, and that was the last he saw of her.

Ref: Helen

T. says he leaves at midnight. Old lady walking about 3 a.m. on Highway 10 between Marshfield and Stevens Point. Two people. Skinny male.

We received an anonymous call from a female subject that she was just at the Mosinee Airport and she stated that she talked to an elderly female that matched the description of Mrs. Kunz. Apparently the female was alone and from what the caller stated, she was wearing a coat and a scarf. The woman stated that she liked gardening and was alone.

I called the security guard and sent a deputy to check. It wasn't her.

Roseville Police Department reported:

Information from one of our citizens. She believed she sighted Helen Kunz in Roseville, Minnesota, at the Bishop's Buffet Restaurant in the Har Mar Mall. She advised that the woman was in her 70s and wearing a long black coat and a scarf. Had blonde or white/gray hair and watery blue eyes.

121

Although unlikely Ms. Kunz would be in Roseville, PD felt it needed to pass the information along.

Re: Possible sighting of "Helen Kunz"
Caller said last night she did observe and talk to an older woman. Caller called her a bag lady. Said this older woman had a few bags with her. Said older woman had short gray hair and large eyes. Caller said this was in the area of the bus station in Bloomington, Minnesota. Caller said she did tell this older woman about an all-night store where she could wait.
Said the older woman was going to Burnsville.

S. reported she saw an older female in her 70s hitch-hiking south on Grand Avenue. Subject had a suitcase.

Tomahawk Police Department received a call from a Tomahawk resident that a woman resembling "Helen" was sitting in a blue Buick Park Avenue in the parking lot of a Tomahawk grocery story.
The witness is a reliable Tomahawk resident, according to the PD.

Owner of the Pointe Resort and Club, Minoqua, reported that when she checked the guest book that they have out for people to sign, there are two entries on July 24, 1987. Dave Kunz and Helen Kunz. Said there were several people in that day and was unable to say who it was that signed the names.

P. says he saw a "Helen look-alike" standing on a street corner in front of Riiser Gas Station. Scarf around her head. Boots on. Looking out of place.

Female caller said that her ex-mother-in-law said that she had heard that Helen had been sighted in the Chicago area by person or persons living in the Cedar Rail Home for the Elderly in

Marshfield. Caller said she did not want get involved, but wanted to pass this info on.

Sheriff,

A woman was in this morning wanting to talk to you. She claims she has seen Helen in a black Blazer with a gray stripe with a man with long black hair in Wausau. She has seen the Blazer again near the Christian Book Store. She reeked of alcohol and I think she was a quart low. I told her I would tell you about it and that she should call me if she thinks she sees Helen again.

Caller said she had a vision of where Helen was buried. Caller said she couldn't sleep last night. After she had this vision, it bothered her all day. She said she would like to talk to someone about this.

Caller claims she went to bed this evening and had a vision. She saw a vehicle at a swamp. The vehicle was red and white. The vehicle faced southeast. The swamp was on the left.

She saw a person who was blurred. She didn't know if it was a man or a female, but thought it was a male. She had the feeling that it was someone who had lived with the Kunz family—like a foster child.

She had the feeling it was sex-related.

For some of those who reported visions and sightings to the Marathon County Sheriff's Department, Helen seemed to have become a depository of their own hurt, pain, family torment and desire for revenge.

Dear Sheriff Schillinger,

I want to write to you about Helen Kunz. For two months I have been debating whether I want to do this, but I feel compelled to do so. Because I think I know what happened and the reasons for the shocking murders committed by Helen Kunz on the night of July Fourth.

Helen Kunz is alive and will return to the scene of the crime in the near future. She cannot stay away. Meanwhile I cannot understand how she is surviving.

Helen was not a bad person.

In fact, she was kind, sensitive and had been a very good mother to both her sons; she did not abandon them. In fact, she doted on her younger son, and gave him everything possible. But Randy had a mean streak in him, and it bordered on the sadistic. He often taunted his mother, and did not appreciate things she did for him.

Helen liked going out, away from the farm. She would much rather go out than have company, because some of the relatives ridiculed her (for having two illegitimate sons) and I think she would rather work in her garden than participate in visiting.

Basically, Helen was an incurable romantic.

Many times she had considered leaving the farm, going to the city, and finding something out there she could never have on the farm. But she didn't leave. "You owe us," they said. She stayed. Worked in her garden, did the shopping, paid the bills, and had a few friends outside. I doubt she ever wrote letters to friends. I think she liked to read love stories and watch romantic movies.

There was so little of that in her life, so she lived on dreams.

Helen and Randy returned from the fireworks around 10:40 in the evening. They argued in the kitchen about TV watching, and for once in her life, she forbade her son to turn on the TV to watch pornographic films. She became so angry, she fought him, and he pushed her against a wall. The result was that she grabbed an axe, near the wood-box, and struck him in the head with the blunt end of it.

He fell. Aghast, she dashed up the stairs to her room to get her handgun. Coming back to the kitchen, she passed the open door to Clarence's room, and she went in and shot him as he lay sleeping. For years, she had nothing but contempt for him and was very sorry she had ever let her older brother take liberties with her when she was a young girl.

Coming through the living room, she saw Irene dozing in her favorite chair. Perhaps she was waiting for the TV to come on. Helen shot her, too.

Going back into the kitchen, she hardly looked at her son, Randy, who may or may not have been already dead, but she shot him too.

Then her sister Marie stood in the doorway (she had been awakened by all the noise) and she stood wide-eyed with her hands over her mouth and stared at Helen.

She rushed at Helen and threatened to phone the police. Helen got to the phone ahead of her and ripped the wires from the wall. Helen ran from the room and out to the porch, while Marie ran after her. Marie was shot and killed on the porch steps.

Then Helen ran away.

Perhaps she tried to start Randy's car, but she had never driven a car. She did succeed in moving it a short distance., but it stalled and she got out and walked. Helen was trembling and sick.

The above is my theory, Mr. Schillinger. Do not call me a psychic. I am not in the habit of following murder stories, or even reading them. But something compelled me to get interested in this case.

When you find her, be kind to Helen.

She will not kill again.

Sincerely,

another Helen (age 66)

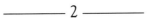

——— 2 ———

From a letter to the Catholic Welfare Bureau, from the state Division for Children and Youth, dated Jan. 2, 1957:

Dear Reverend:

St. Joseph's Hospital at Marshfield, Wis., reported to this department the admission on 12–29–56 of Helen Catherine Kunz, single and of the white race. Her religion is Catholic. She gave birth to a boy on 12–29–56.

May we refer this case to you in order that this girl may be given assistance in making constructive plans for herself and baby?

From a medical report, filed by Helen Kunz's physician, on March 13, 1953:

Acquaintance made of patient. Simple personality. Patient believes she is pregnant. Wishes she was married. Never had a boyfriend. "Mother wouldn't let me." 7th grade in school. "Very hard, but I can read and write."

Wears wedding band on left 4th finger. Denies sexual activity.

Patient continues to complain of bizarre hot feeling in abdomen, not a pain, connected with idea of being pregnant. She is menstruating now, but this does not cancel the thought of pregnancy in her mind.

Patient has been closest, of all her sisters, to her brother. She went to school with him. So is probably very protective of him and feels guilt for anything they could have been involved in together.

Believe patient has mild mental deficiency (moron). Humble personality. Believe patient will show gradual improvement and may go home when motivated to.

Helen was 39 and Kenny was 23 when Randy was born four days after Christmas in 1956.

In her blue purse, the one with the vinyl strap, the one she hung on a peg in the storage room, Helen Kunz kept the following items:

—$122.40

—Several money order receipts, including two—one to Valentine Products, Inc., and another to Instant Action, Inc.—which had been used to purchase pornographic materials for Randy.

—A renewal notice from the Hitchcock Mystery Magazine, with the space for extending the current subscription checked "yes."

—A renewal notice from the National Rifle Association and the American Rifleman. They were in an NRA business reply envelope, together with $25 in cash.

—Randy Kunz's driver's license, expiration date 12/29/87.

When Detectives Roddy and Hoenisch drove out to Athens High School, neither was very surprised to learn that very few faculty members remembered Randy.

"He was pretty much of a loner," said Jim Rogaczewski, a guidance counselor.

One exception was Gary Beastrom, who taught Randy vocational agriculture in the 9th and 10th grades. Beastrom was also a member of the Athens ambulance crew, and had been following the case closely.

"I guess you'd say he was pretty average. Never caused any problems," Beastrom said.

"He always sat at the front of the class, at the very end of the table so he wouldn't have students sitting on both sides. His hygiene wasn't what it should have been. His hair was long, but not in a fashionable way. Just uncut. And his clothes were sort of out of style and unclean. Sometimes his body odor would be pretty awful."

"Did the other students pick on him?" Roddy asked.

"Not that I ever saw," Beastrom said.

"I can tell you two stories about Randy that have always sort of stuck in my mind.

"The class had this garden project—you know, they were supposed to keep a garden and a record of how it was doing. So, one day I drove out to the Kunz place. Randy met me at my car and wouldn't give me a chance to get out.

"Not that I wanted to. There were dogs everywhere. And Randy looked very uneasy about me coming out to his house.

"It was a big switch from the Randy I knew at school. Randy was pretty friendly to me at school. But at the house, he clearly wanted me to go away. I figured he was embarrassed about something. Fine. I left.

"The other thing is this—this happened, oh eight, ten years ago. After Randy was out of school.

"There's this guy west of Athens who's got a beautiful herd of registered Guernseys. He pastured his cows on one side of the road and milked them on another. He had signs up and all warning folks about this patch of road being a cattle crossing, and he would stand in the road himself and guard his animals when he had to bring them across.

"So one afternoon, Randy is driving his mother to an Athens High football game and just plows through this guy's herd. One animal got its leg broke and had to be destroyed.

"Randy didn't even slow down. Just keeps driving.

"So the dairy farmer gets in his car and follows them out to the high school. There's Helen and Randy, fixing to watch the game.

"The farmer was pretty hacked off, but what could he do? From what I understand, the Kunzes paid for the animal."

On their way out, Hoenisch picked of a copy of the 1984 yearbook with Randy and Helen's picture in it.

"Education is the Key to Success," it said.

As they drove back to Wausau, Hoenisch read Roddy the yearbook's closing quote:

"Teenagers are like engines, and somehow you end up with the ignition keys to some of them and you start them up, but you don't know what they are or what they're supposed to do. There are clues, but that's all. A summer job generates new interests, or a trip, or a course in school. Engines. They give you the keys and some clues and they say, 'Start it up, see what it will do,' and sometimes what it does is pull you along into a life that's really good and fulfilling, and sometimes what it does is pull you right down the highway to loneliness and regret, and it leaves you all alone and deserted by the roadside."

"There's a cheerful thought," Roddy said. "Where'd that come from?"

"*Christine*," Hoenisch said. "You know, that Steven King book about the homicidal car."

"Oh yeah," Roddy said. "Homicidal car. Right."

Roddy and Hoenisch were not having an easy time figuring out what kind of relationship Helen had with Randy.

Sure, they did everything together: They slept together, they ate together, went to basketball games together. When Helen had to do the laundry, Randy drove her to town, then waited for her in his car. When she did the shopping, there was Randy, waiting in the car.

It had been years since anyone remembered seeing the two apart.

A high school buddy recalled that Randy came to his class's 10th reunion and that Randy had danced with a couple of girls. He said Randy left alone and that he hadn't seen him since.

Went home to his mamma, Hoenisch thought.

To Helen.

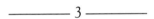

————— 3 —————

It pissed off Hoenisch more than just a little.

Schillinger came strolling into the office with this goofy grin on his face, sat on the edge of Hoenisch's desk and stared at him. Smiling. Not saying a word.

"Yes?" Hoenisch said.

"You're not looking," Schillinger said. It had been eight days since the Kunz murders were discovered. Ten to 15 detectives had been working around the clock, often pulling double shifts as they interviewed potential witnesses, sat through stakeouts, went to court seeking search warrants, touched base with the media, searched corn fields and garbage bins, filed reports. And they had nothing. Not much anyway. Hoenisch was tired.

"See?" Schillinger said. He pointed to a bright pink button he had pinned to the lapel of his navy blue jacket.

It said "Where's Helen?"

"Some woman was selling them downtown this weekend. One buck."

Hoenisch thought: "Wait'll the media gets a load of that."

From *The Milwaukee Sentinel*
July 14, 1987:

Sheriff Says Buttons
May Aid Hunt for Kunz

The sale of buttons reading "Where's Helen?" was supported Monday by Marathon County Sheriff LeRoy Schillinger, who said the buttons might help investigators find Helen Kunz, 70, who has been missing since four of her relatives were found slain July 5.

Roddy waited in the car while Hoenisch knocked on Germaine's door. The door opened a crack, Germaine peeked out, and then pushed it shut again. Hoenisch could hear the chain lock rattle, then the door opened wide and Kenny stepped out.

"I'm ready I guess to go," he said.

The three drove to Wausau, first to the Wausau Hospital Center emergency room, where a doctor took 20 cc of blood, then to the Sheriff's Department, where a deputy took Kenny's picture, clipped some hair from his head and made a complete set of fingerprints.

"I know you think I had something to do with this," Kenny told Roddy. "I didn't. Not at all."

Roddy tended to believe Kenny, but he and Hoenisch continued to pressure him throughout the day.

"Who else?" Roddy asked him. "Who could have been involved in this?"

Kenny had just finished washing the ink off his fingers, and he didn't seem to be paying attention. Roddy sat down at his desk and felt vaguely nauseated.

"It could have been these fellows who came out about two years ago. Year and a half ago, maybe."

"Who? How many fellows?"

"Four from Medford," Kenny said. "Four fellows came to the house. They wanted to buy two cars. '75 Ford. '69 Oldsmobile."

"What were their names?" Hoenisch asked. He was jotting it all down in his notebook.

Kenny shrugged.

"Two older—maybe in their 20s. One was tall with black hair. One was tall and blond and wore glasses. He was tall too. The other two were kids. Teenagers."

"Did they come in the house?" Hoenisch asked.

"Why I remember it is because they came in the house while I searched for the titles. Then, after they left, I noticed some things were missing."

"What was missing?"

"Calculator from the table. Funnel from entry way. Chain from garage. East Medford. Somewhere around East Medford is where they were from."

"What did they pay with?" Roddy asked. "Do you remember what they paid with?"

"Check."

"Okay, Kenny. What was the name on the check?"

Kenny closed his eyes.

"Don't remember. But maybe if I think. I called the number on the check and said to the one he stole my things. I told him I would call the police if he didn't bring them back."

"What was the name of the person you called, Kenny?"

Kenny shook his head.

"Don't remember. He brought the stuff back. The tall one with the dark hair."

"Did you see them again?"

131

"Not—Helen. Helen did. Not me. Helen says about a month ago one of the four came by. Helen didn't trust him 'cause of the things getting stole. He wants to buy '65 Chevy. Been sitting out there a long time. But Helen says talk to Kenny."

"Did you? Talk to him?"

"Never heard from him again."

"Whose name was on the check. Think hard, Kenny."

Kenny said he would.

Kenny rode in the front seat beside Roddy as they drove back toward Abbotsford. Kenny wiped his fingers back and forth across the knees of his pants.

"Bank of Athens," he said. "I remember the check was from Bank of Athens."

"Okay, Kenny. Who wrote the check?"

"Let's see. Jacobs. It was Jacobs. I won't remember the first name. Maybe I will. But the last name on the the check was Jacobs."

Part III

CHRIS

I would like to fling my voice out like a cloth
over the fragments of your death, and keep
pulling at it until it is torn to pieces,
and all my words would have to walk around
shivering, in the tatters of that voice;
if lament were enough. But now I must accuse:
not the man who withdrew you from yourself
(I can not find him; he looks like everyone)
but in this one man, I accuse: all men.

Rainer Maria Rilke
Requiem für eine Freundin

Chapter 1

Smoking Tires

——— 1 ———

Chris J. Jacobs III searched for a bell, and finding none, pounded on the door of the Kunzes' front porch.

A chorus of dogs erupted from inside, and Chris stepped back, thrusting his fingers into the frayed front pockets of his Levi jeans. A moment passed. Then another. The dogs continued to wail.

Jacobs stepped back up to the porch and pounded again, then turned toward the brown Dodge Ram pickup truck parked in the driveway behind him. Crammed into the cab of the truck were four buddies: Billy, Willie, Mike and Mike's 14-year-old brother, Perry.

"C'mon," he yelled.

It was July 1, 1984. Almost dusk. It had rained that afternoon. Hard. Water still dripped from the unguttered eaves of the Kunzes' home, dropping into a narrow puddle that ran the length of the house's roof-line.

Jacobs, still more than four months from his 18th birthday, was already tall and barrel-chested, with thick black hair, a strong hard

135

jaw and movie-star-quality dimples. He wore a grimy white T-shirt, untucked, and a blue work shirt, unbuttoned. His black steel-toed work shoes were scarred and stained with grease. So were his hands.

"C'mon," he yelled.

The truck doors opened and his friends climbed out just as the porch door opened, revealing a small elderly woman—it was Helen—dressed in a long flowered dress, a navy blue sweater and a babushka. A dog rushed past her and into the yard. The rest—three or four—roiled around and around behind her, howling as she held them at bay with the handle of a broom.

"I'm wondering about a car you have," Chris yelled above the dogs.

"The Ford parked out by the weeds there."

Chris pointed to a yellow and black two-door 1969 Oldsmobile Cutlass parked at the end of the driveway.

"I want to buy it. If it's for sale."

"Yes. Okay," the woman said. She smiled. Chris could barely hear her above the dogs. She pointed to Kenny's trailer. "Ask in there. Ask the man in there."

Kenny was hitching up his pants and yanking up its zipper when he opened up the thin door of his trailer. Chris asked him about the car. At first Kenny seemed confused and disturbed by the five teenage boys outside his door, but then agreed to come with them to look at the car.

Chris had seen the car the day before and had stopped by the farm to give it a careful inspection. It was very rusty, but the tires seemed good, and it had four-on-the-floor and a working CB radio. Chris figured he could chop it up and sell the parts for about $200 or so.

"It's a rust-bucket," Chris said. "But I'll give you $50 for it."

Kenny shook his head.

"Starter's broke and it don't hardly run. It'll run, though. Runs rough. I don't think it's worth more than $30."

Chris said, "Fine."

"Come into the house," Kenny said.

The five teenagers crowded into the Kunzes' kitchen. While Helen searched for the title, Chris wrote out a check on his parents' account. Randy came out for a moment, then disappeared into his bedroom. Marie sat in a chair in the living room, just outside the kitchen door. She never spoke. When one of the boys said "hi" to her, she covered her mouth with her hand and smiled. Irene lay on a bed nearby, peeking out from behind a pillow.

All the while, the dogs bayed and Helen kept up a banter no one could hear. She came into the kitchen and opened a metal filing cabinet.

"It's in here, I think," she said.

She pulled out several bundles of cash, each two to three inches thick and held together by three rubber bands, and placed them on top of the cabinet while she rummaged through the drawer.

It wasn't until the next day that Kenny noticed that his calculator, which he always kept on the kitchen table, was missing. So was a chain the boys had borrowed to pull the car out to the road, as well as the funnel they had used to prime the car's carburetor.

One of the boys had left a phone number with Kenny. He called the boy and told him he would call the police. The items were returned the following day.

Within a month, Chris was back, this time with two friends— Jerome and Billy—and this time interested in a 1974 Ford Galaxy 500. It had just clicked 80,000 miles, and it had good tires. Chris wanted the engine for a '31 Ford pickup he was fixing up. Kenny asked $20 for it. Chris paid him in cash.

"How about a little gas so's I can get this thing home," Chris asked.

Kenny shook his head.

" 'Cause you see $20 isn't so much," Kenny said. He was still peeved that they had stolen some of his things.

"I need just a little gas," Chris said. "C'mon."

Kenny shrugged. He went into the pole barn and came out with a 5-gallon can of gas. He poured the contents into the Ford.

"Okay well then there you go," Kenny said. "There you go."

The three boys jump-started the car. Chris was afraid the engine would stall if he took his foot off the gas pedal, so Billy climbed into the passenger seat and they took off, with Jerome following them in Chris's gold Dodge Charger.

It was mid-afternoon. Dry and a tad cool. Yolk-colored plumes of road dust billowed from behind the cars as they sped over gravel roads, between fields of corn, alfalfa and wheat.

Jerome could hardly see where he was driving. He just followed Chris, speeding faster and faster. Then, in the dust, he saw a stop sign, perhaps 50 yards ahead. He began to brake and downshift and the car shimmied to a halt, just at the lip of a paved county highway, just a foot or two beyond the stop sign, just as a tanker truck hauling milk blew by, missing the nose of his car by inches.

Jerome crossed the road. Up ahead, Chris was spinning the Ford in circles, one after another, until it came up facing Jerome. Jerome slowed his car, then Chris took off, speeding down the road in reverse until the front end hooked backward, and the car went careening into a ditch.

Billy, his glasses hanging from one ear, scrambled out.

"God-damn-jesus-h-christ," he yelled. "You could have fucking killed us, Chris, you crazy god-damn-son-of-a-bitch!"

But Chris couldn't hear him.

He was standing, one foot on the brake and one foot on the gas pedal, his hands gripping the steering wheel, his back arched over the seat, roaring over the roar of the smoking tires, roaring and smoking the tires until the car ran out of gas.

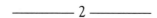

———— 2 ————

After Roddy and Hoenisch dropped Kenny off at Germaine's house, they drove to the Bank of Athens to see if anyone held a checking account there under the name "Jacobs."

A man punched some letters into a computer.

"Yes," he said. "Chris Jacobs, Jr., N3984 Martin Drive. That's just a few miles north of here. Near Medford."

The detectives added Chris Jacobs's name to their list of people they needed to interview. It was a good tip, one of ten dozen they would get to as soon as possible.

Toward the end of July, two brothers—Patrick and Daniel Harding— were fishing the Big Rib River north of Athens when they smelled something awful.

"I'll never forget the smell," Patrick later recalled.

"It was like a sweet, rotting stench—like nothing I have ever smelled before."

The stench drove the two boys off the river. As they were walking back to their truck, they saw a dark-colored pickup stop on the bridge ahead. Two men got out, looked down the river in their direction, then started walking toward the Hardings' truck. As the boys got closer, the two men turned back to their truck and took off.

That night, Patrick's and Daniel's parents grilled steaks in their backyard. Patrick said he couldn't eat his.

On a hot August morning, little more than a month after the murders, Kenny Kunz and his friend, Ken Fasse, went up to the Kunzes' house to weed out the garden.

Fasse ran a tiller between the rows of onions, cucumbers, peas, beans, tomatoes, zucchini, cabbage and corn, while Kenny picked anything that seemed worth taking.

Since the killings, the garden had been left unwatered and untended, and the ground was hard and cracked. The yellow tape investigators had used to set up a police line drooped between trees and bushes. Kenny stopped and opened a beer.

His wore a camouflage hat, pulled low over his eyes, and a blue work shirt stained with sweat. He put the cool beer can against the vein on the side of his neck, then bent to pick a cucumber.

"Small," he said.

"Good for pickles."

Kenny's harvest seemed plentiful compared to the leads Detectives Roddy and Hoenisch were able to glean from the mass of tips that flooded the Sheriff's department daily.

Some were just kooky, such as a letter they received from an inmate at the state prison who suggested a few angles, then ended: "I'll be out 3-30-90. If nothing is found out more about this case, would you mind if I had a go at it? Just because I'm away doesn't mean Wausau isn't my home town."

Or this, from a guy who signed his name, "Sherlock Holmes":

"Just a little clu for all you sheriffs & FBI on the loose.

"Those trained dogs & bloodhounds have a real good sniffer & really know how to track us down. But then you just might find out who it is we did it."

There was a whole class of letters and phone calls from people who described themselves as psychics. They recounted weird dreams of flying over farmland, visions of Helen's body hidden beneath sheets of aluminum siding, odd feelings evoked by farm implements and animals.

One woman wrote about her mother in Sioux Falls, South Dakota, who, at the daughter's urging, went into a trance:

"I asked her who murdered these people.

"The answer I received was this: 'Someone who is an excellent marksman. One who can fire many times in a row without missing.'"

Another class of letters came from people interested in getting their neighbors in trouble:

"Just want to pass this name along in regards to these homicides in Marathon County. Have no idea where this individual lives and he probably had nothing to do with it (The letter-writer then offers a name.)

"just a name wanted to pass on don't care to give my name is i don't feel i'd enough or any much basis to mention this name in reguard to these matters. but as a concerned citizen ifeel some sort of duty to mention this."

Sheriff Schillinger had a few theories of his own, which he shared one day with Milwaukee Sentinel reporter Peter Maller as the two ate lunch at a cafe a few blocks from the Marathon County Jail.

"I think Helen Kunz is alive," Schillinger said. He took a bite of his egg salad sandwich and looked around the nearly empty dining room.

It was a hunch, he told Maller, based on hundreds of pieces of evidence and by a three-inch stack of reports filed by his investigators.

"But it's hard for me to put my theory out in public at this time," he said. "You can't divulge your theory, or it may blow the whole thing apart."

Schillinger's remarks—extraordinarily indiscreet for a man in charge of an investigation as high-profile as the Kunz murders—resulted in a front page story in the Sentinel, frustration among the department's rank-and-file, and an angry letter to Roddy from Germaine's daughter:

"We, the family of Helen Kunz, are very disturbed over the last two reports in the newspapers.

"Is Sheriff Schillinger trying to keep the Helen Kunz name in the spotlight—or his own name? His saying that he is sure Helen is still alive is like a little first-grader taunting, 'Ha! Ha! I know something you don't know!'

"We really do expect a little more responsible reporting and surely hope he is not speaking for the whole department. We feel this a terrible tragedy and not the humorous affair that it seems to be treated by the sheriff's remarks.

"And we feel that we, the family members (the living and the dead), deserve a little more consideration and respect and compassion."

Roddy and Hoenisch were beset by theories, but still no solid leads, no pattern, no breaks had emerged.

Then, in early November, Athens Police Chief Pat Ostrowski mentioned to Hoenisch that he had a suspect in the burglary of some car parts dating back to March.

"A kid named Chris Jacobs," Ostrowski said. "Kind of a trouble-maker. Ever hear of him?"

A few days after that, Roddy got a phone call from Norm Dassow, a Sheriff's deputy in neighboring Taylor County, who was investigating a Nov. 4 burglary and car theft.

"Have you guys come across the name 'Chris Jacobs?'" he asked.

——— 3 ———

From a Taylor County Sheriff's Department report, filed by Deputy Norm Dassow:

> On Wednesday, November 4, 1987, officer was contacted by Randall Faber.
> Faber informed the officer that he had his car stored in his dad's garage and sometime during the previous night someone broke in and took it. The garage is owned by Norbert E. Faber.
> In talking with Norbert Faber, officer was informed that he left the garage on November 3, at 10 a.m., and returned at approximately 12:30 p.m. on November 4 and found that someone broke in and took the below described vehicle:
> 1973 Dodge Charger, 2 door. Vehicle is black vinyl over red in color, has orange and black stripes on each side. Vehicle is equipped with a 426 Hemmy Engine. It has N50s tires on the rear. Value: $7,500.

Everyone who knew Chris Jacobs knew he loved Dodge Chargers.

He had owned three or four of them even before he had his driver's license, and he had owned 17 Chargers before he was 20. At the time of the Faber theft, Chris was driving a Charger his father had bought new in 1974. By the time Mr. Jacobs gave the car to his son in 1984, the car was rusty and worn-out. Chris restored it, painted it black, added orange stripes along its sides.

"Super-sharp," Chris said.

The Jacobses owned two pieces of property.

The first, about 93 acres, was in the Town of Bern, in Marathon County, about seven miles northeast of the Kunzes' place and about seven miles northwest of Athens.

Chris lived with his parents—Chris Jr. and Judith—in a little white house on the Town of Bern property. There was a barn and a silo out back, and a statue of an eagle mounted on the lawn out front. In the summer, daisies covered the front lawn.

The Town of Bern farm faced North Town Line Road, which marked the northern boundary of Marathon County and the southern boundary of Taylor County.

The Jacobses owned an additional 192 acres of land in the Town of Goodrich, less than 15 miles north of their Town of Bern home. The Town of Goodrich farm had a vacant house and several buildings used for dairy farming.

The north farm was cater-cornered from the Fabers' place, and about five miles from where the Harding brothers were fishing when they smelled that awful smell.

From a Taylor County Sheriff's Department report filed by Deputy Dassow:

On Tuesday, Nov. 10, officer contacted Chris Jacobs at the Jacobs' north farm. The officer was assisted by Marathon County Detectives Roddy and Hoenisch and Chief of Police Pat Ostrowski.

Chris Jacobs readily agreed to allow the officers to conduct an informal search of the farm. Officers were allowed access to the house by Chris Jacobs.

While in the house, Detective Roddy and Chief Ostrowski made a check of the upstairs. While upstairs they observed a dashboard, black in color, bearing VIN #WH23U3G148746.

Officers then compared the VIN number which was observed on the dashboard to that of the report made by Randy O. Faber on Nov. 4.

The two VIN numbers were the same.

From a Marathon County Sheriff's Department report filed by Detective Roddy:

On November 13, 1987, I and three other Marathon County detectives met Deputy Dassow on the highway south of the Jacobses' Town of Goodrich farm. Dassow advised me that he had a search warrant for the house where we observed the dash only. He also advised me that he had an arrest warrant for Christopher J. Jacobs III for the theft of the dash of the Dodge Charger.

While we were on our way to the farm, we met Chris Jacobs heading south. Officer Dassow waved Chris down and he stopped and returned to the farm with us.

Chris unlocked the house for us to search. He asked that he be allowed to drive to the home farm, as he had milk in the back of his truck. Deputy Dassow followed Chris back to the home farm.

We searched the house. The dash that had been there on Tuesday was gone. Two detectives followed some tracks out into a field east of the building and located a backhoe with a transmission in the bucket and also a pile of dirt from fresh digging that was by the backhoe.

They also observed some fresh red paint chips from the putty of the red vehicle.

Chris and Dassow returned to the farm. Chris's mother and father also came. Chris advised us that the vehicle he was looking for was buried out by the backhoe.

When they got the car out of the hole, we found that the motor and transmission and all had been removed from the vehicle, the hood, front fenders and doors were also removed along with the dashboard. About the only thing left on the vehicle itself were the four tires and rims.

The car had been dumped in the hole and the car actually folded in half.

From a confession, signed by Chris Jacobs:

> The main reason I took the car was to get the engine. I was
> probably drunk at the time.

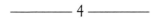

— 4 —

The first snows came, followed by an early-winter thaw. With
the leaves of the trees and the underbrush thinned, Roddy and
Hoenisch decided to spend an afternoon searching the Kunzes' farm
for anything that might have been missed in July

The door was opened to the house and they found Kenny sitting
in the kitchen, rubbing a dog behind its ears.

"Hey, Kenny," Roddy said.

A large black cat stepped out from behind the door. There was
a bowl of fresh cream set out in front of the stove. Beside it was a plate
of dog food.

"Some of the animals are still here," Kenny said. "I try to get by.
You know. To feed them."

From a Marathon County Sheriff's Department report filed by
Detective Roddy:

> On November 25, 1987, Detective Hoenisch and I went to
> the Kraft Plant in Milan and interviewed Eileen Moore, manager.
>
> There is one big change in Kenneth Kunz, and that is that
> before the murders of his family, he never did attend any company
> functions. Eileen Moore said that now he attends any company
> function and stays. He is now one of the last ones to leave.

Meteorologists called it a Siberian Express: a frigid weather
pattern that formed on the desolate Siberian plains, then swept west,
across Canada and down into the Midwest, hitting Marathon
County during the first week of 1988.

Temperatures dropped to 25 below zero, and wind-chills dropped to 40 below.

In Stratford, helpless firefighters watched as a fire destroyed a home; the front-mounted pump on their engine had frozen. In Wausau, a man and woman were overcome by carbon monoxide when their chimney froze shut. Batteries died. Radiators exploded.

Then came the snow storm, the worse in a decade. Ten inches to a foot fell in a single day, shutting down schools and airports, blocking roads, and sending the Sheriff's Department into a frenzy as deputies worked day and night to check on shut-ins, rescue stranded snowmobilers, open roads and manage what seemed to be an endless barrage of car accidents, great and small.

The Wausau Daily Herald picked the Kunz murders as the top story of 1987 and recapped the slayings in a front-page story headlined: "Where's Helen?"

Roddy and Hoenisch had no idea. A promising lead would come in, only to prove to be a dead-end.

The Luna County Sheriff's Department in Deming, New Mexico, sent a Teletype saying they found the body of an elderly woman fitting Helen's description. Roddy called and asked them to check the woman's hands and teeth.

Hands were normal; no enlarged joints. Teeth were well-kept. Dead-end.

The most promising clues seemed to be the tire tracks investigators found around the Kunzes's garden on July 5.

By examining the tracks, Roddy and Hoenisch could tell several things.

First, the tracks came from three cars. One set of tracks matched the tires on Kenny's car. That would be consistent with his claim that he had been to the garden July 4, rototilling until about 9:30 p.m.

The second came from Randy's car, which was found on the north side of the garden, behind a row of corn. The investigators had no idea why the car was at the garden, rather than the Kunzes' house a quarter of mile away.

The third set of tracks came from an unidentified car.

There was something else Roddy and Hoenisch could tell by studying the tire tracks: because of the way the tracks crossed over each other, they could determine the sequence in which they were made.

First Kenny's car made a set of tracks when he arrived at the garden. His car made another set when he departed, sometime around 9:30 p.m.

Next, the unidentified car made a set of tracks when it arrived.

Then, Randy's car made a set of tracks when it arrived. Helen and Randy were last seen at the Athens fireworks between 10 and 10:30 p.m., so those tracks had to have been made after then. Randy's car, of course, never pulled back out.

Then, the unidentified car made another set of tracks when it departed.

In early January, Roddy and Hoenisch packed up the photographs, the plaster casts that were taken of the tire impressions, and the maps they made of the tracks and the garden, and brought them down to the State Crime Laboratory in Madison.

The Crime Lab has tread design guides for virtually every tire ever manufactured. It was immediately evident that the two front tires matched and that the two rear tires matched, but that the front tires were a different brand from the rear tires.

The two detectives pored through the tread design guides and went home certain that the front tires of the unidentified car were some kind of BF Goodrich belted T/A's.

They were fairly certain that the rear tires were Duralon DS Premium Polyester tires.

Goodrich belted T/A's come in various sizes, as well as various ratios.

There is the 70 series, which means that the tire is 70% as high as it is wide, and there is the 60 series, which means that the tire is 60% as high as it is wide.

Roddy, who had once worked in a garage, brought home several design guides, studied them, and concluded that tires that made the tracks through the Kunzes' garden were in the 70 series.

A few days later, the two detectives drove to Eau Claire, where they met with a product engineer at the UniRoyal-Goodrich plant. He confirmed that the front tires were Goodrich belted T/A's.

Only one store in the area sold BF Goodrich tires: Mason & Sims Tire City, located right across the street from the County Courthouse in Wausau.

"This particular tire your asking about isn't very popular," Mel Sims told the detectives. "They have something of a following among young people."

Sims checked through his sales invoices. In the past five years, he had sold two BF Goodrich belted T/A 70 series tires in 1983, four in 1984, none in 1985, two in 1986 and none in 1987.

"Can you tell me who you sold those tires to in 1986?" Roddy asked.

"Sure," Mel said. He pulled the invoice out of a file cabinet and handed it Roddy. Roddy looked it over and handed it to Hoenisch.

It said: "Chris Jacobs."

According to the invoice, Chris had purchased four Goodrich belted T/A's on March 10, 1986. Two of them had been in the 70 series and two had been in the 60 series. Most likely the 70 series, being smaller, would have been installed on the front and the 60 series installed on the back.

"That's the way the younger generation likes to run them," Mel said.

On Friday, Jan. 22, Chris Jacobs was arraigned in Taylor County Circuit Court, where he was charged with stealing Faber's Dodge Charger.

Chris pleaded no contest to one count of felony theft. Reserve Circuit Judge Karl Peplau accepted the plea and found Chris guilty as charged. The judge continued Chris's $2,000 cash bond and ordered a pre-sentence report.

The hearing, which began at 1:30 p.m., lasted barely an hour.

Across the street from the courthouse, in the parking lot of Chris's attorney, Roddy and Hoenisch crouched in the snow beside Chris's black 1974 Dodge Charger.

Mounted on the front, they found BF Goodrich belted T/A's. On the back, they found Duralon DS Premium Polyesters.

Chapter 2

Thin Ice

1

Roddy and Hoenisch had a suspect, but they didn't have a case.

All they could prove was that a vehicle with an unusual configuration of tires, a configuration matching the tires on the car Chris Jacobs drove to court five months later, had stopped at the Kunzes' garden—a full quarter of a mile from the Kunzes' house—on the night of the murders.

Roddy and Hoenisch were confident that forensics would be able to prove that it was Chris's own car that made the tracks.

But they had no proof that Chris was driving the car. They had no proof that, even if it was Chris driving the car, that he went up to the Kunzes' house. They had no proof that, even if it was Chris driving the car, that he was the one who executed three, perhaps four, elderly people and a shy, harmless 30-year-old man.

Roddy and Hoenisch had a suspect, but they did not have what they would need to convince a jury, beyond a reasonable doubt, that it should send a 21-year-old boy away to prison for the rest of his life.

Besides, the detectives doubted that the Kunz family slayings were the work of a lone killer.

The magnitude of the crime and the efficient manner in which it was carried off were indicative of that. And there was something else.

Roddy and Hoenisch had interviewed a witness who said that on the night of the killings, she drove by the Kunzes' house on her way to work.

It was about 10 or 10:30 p.m., she said, when, while traveling north, she reached an intersection a short distance from the Kunzes' place. Just then, a vehicle parked on the north side of the intersection turned on its bright lights, as well as a spotlight on the right-hand side of the vehicle.

The lights blinded her for a moment, but she drove on. She glanced into her rear-view mirror and saw that the vehicle had begun to follow her.

As she neared the Kunzes' house, she began to slow down. She did so out of habit. The Kunzes kept so many dogs that she was afraid, particularly at night, that she might run one over. Just then, the vehicle that had been following her pulled up tight behind her and someone began shining the spotlight into her car.

But then, after she passed the Kunzes' house, the vehicle behind her slowed. In her mirror, she watched it stop and turn around.

The woman's car was very similar to Kenny's car, and Roddy figured that the driver of the vehicle with the spotlight was a lookout, watching to see when Kenny would come home.

It was early Friday morning, Jan. 29.

Warm moist air had moved over the region and a thick fog covered the ground. Chris Jacobs was working his chores at the north farm, getting ready to put out some feed for the cattle, when he heard a car coming up the driveway. Chris looked out the window of the barn, and seeing that the car contained Roddy and Hoenisch, he wiped his hands on his jeans and went out to see what the officers wanted.

"Heard you might have bought a car or two from the Kunzes," Roddy said. "We've been, you know, trying to talk to everybody that's ever had any contact with those people, so I was wondering if you'd mind telling us about that. If you have the time."

Chris said sure and climbed into the back seat with Hoenisch, who placed a tape recorder on the shelf beneath the rear window and turned it on.

Chris talked about buying the cars from the Kunzes, about his family, his friends, his schooling. The detectives let the conversation ramble.

"When you were there, do you remember seeing a lot of cats and dogs?" Hoenisch asked.

"Yeah. There were dogs there."

"A lot of them? You have any idea about how many were there?"

"Three. Four. Five. I don't know."

"Did they seem pretty mean?"

"Yeah. They were barking like a son-of-a-bitch," Chris said. The two officers smiled. Chris smiled with them.

"They weren't biting," Chris said. "They were barking. You'd keep your distance, you know. Like you'd kind of move away, and they'd come at you, then they'd stop. You know how that is? I don't know."

"We heard at one time they had like close to 20 dogs. Twenty dogs at one time, plus all the cats," Hoenisch said.

"Yeah," Roddy said. "One guy said he had to get rid of about 17 of them—something like that."

"They had to get rid of 17 dogs?" Chris asked. "Why?"

"Nobody could even go near there, it was so bad at one time," Roddy said. "They just let them multiply, you know."

"I know they were barking like a son-of-a-bitch," Chris said. "I didn't pay much attention. I was after that goddamn car."

"Yeah," Hoenisch said. "Well, after I saw your name on that title, I thought it would be a good chance to come up and talk to you about that deal, and also check with you just for the heck of it. Being as young as you are, you got to run into a lot of young guys around here and know them. Most of them are guys that are familiar to you."

There was a pause, then Hoenisch asked, "When did you first hear about what happened down there at that house?"

"Monday morning. Mom and Dad told me about it in the morning."

Chris had a bit of a cold. He rubbed his nose on his sleeve and sniffed.

"What did they say? Do you remember?"

"They told me there had been some murders there by Athens."

"Did they tell you the name of the people?"

"No. I don't know. I heard it the next day on the radio or something. Cause we . . ."

"Did it click as to maybe that's the people you bought the car from?"

"Not at first there. I thought it was Kraus, or Kroutz, I bought 'em from. Something like that."

"Later did it click?"

Chris looked like he was getting uncomfortable.

"Yeah," he said. "I don't know. I don't know. I think they showed the picture of the yard on the thing there, and I sit there thinking. Then it dawned on me then."

"On TV you saw it?"

"Yeah," Chris said. Sniffed. "You guys didn't want to drive in the barn here for a minute, did you?"

"Oh," Hoenisch said. "Look, if you got something to do, you can go ahead."

"I got to take down the silo unloader."

"Sure," Roddy said. "Here, let me let you out."

A few minutes later, Chris came out of the barn looking upset.

"Fucking silo loader sheared off a pin," he said as he got into the back-seat.

"You got to throw it down by hand then?" Roddy asked.

"No. I got to fix the pin. It ain't that bad. I fed the cows hay."

"If it's not long, maybe you'd rather do it now," Roddy said. "We don't want to hold you up on your work here. You got time to sit and talk a little yet?"

Chris sighed. "Yeah."

"We were talking about what you had heard about what had happened down there. Your mom and dad mentioned it to you on Monday . . ."

"I think it was Monday. I don't know. We were up at the cabin partying then, with my friends. Faber's cabin. Don't say too much about it 'cause there's minors that go down there."

"You were partying then—Monday—when you heard it?"

Chris nodded.

"Is that something you did all weekend for the Fourth of July?"

"No. Fourth of July I went to Medford and watched the fireworks."

"You were up in Medford?" Hoenisch said. "So was I."

Chris looked at him.

"I didn't see you," Chris said. "You were off duty, right?"

"No," Hoenisch said. "As a matter of fact, I was up there helping Medford on a deal up there."

"Oh. I'm glad I didn't see you," Chris said. He laughed. The laugh ended with a cough.

"Who were you at the Medford fireworks with?" Roddy asked.

"Um, Annette Harley. We just basically stayed in the car and kind of watched the fireworks and got drunk."

"Who was it?" Roddy asked.

"Annette Harley."

"Your girlfriend?"

"Ah, no. No. No."

Roddy felt Chris was lying. He began to press him for details.

"Where you up there before dark, before it started, or were you there for the whole thing?"

"We got up there just before it was starting."

"It must have been just about dark then?"

"Yeah. Just about."

"How long did it last."

"I don't know. About half an hour. I don't know. I never really sat down and timed it. No, it couldn't have been that long."

"It was just the two of you?"

"Yeah."

"Her car or your car?

"My car."

"The Charger?"

"Yeah."

The conversation drifted to a discussion of Chris's car, then to former friends and to former jobs. The detectives let it drift for a while, then turned it back to July 4.

"I was going to ask you about the fireworks, since I couldn't remember," Hoenisch said.

"I know I saw them up in Medford, but what time—do you remember what time those got over with?"

"Gee, I was feeling really good that night. I was super pissed up."

"Do you remember what you did after the fireworks?"

"Well, we stayed there for the dance for a minute. And, shit. I just took off and went home then."

"Did Annette go home with you?"

"No. She went to her place."

"Where was the dance at?"

"In Medford there. Um. I don't know. In that park deal. I don't know."

"Was it outside?"

"Yeah."

"Kind of like a pavilion or something?"

"I don't know what it was."

"A shelter of some kind?"

"Yeah. I think so. I don't know. I was just betting on pretty much standing by then."

"What kind of music did they have? Was it a band? Was it a disc jockey?"

"Um, I think it was a band."

"It was a live band?"

"Pretty sure it was."

"And they played rock music?"

"Yeah. I don't know. I never walked up there. We stayed down there by the river there pretty much. I was almost getting lucky there for a minute."

"That's what you were working, hey?" Roddy said. He was being Chris's pal. Chris responded.

"It was more fun than dancing. I almost got lucky that time, too. That I can remember in the morning. I had a smile on my face all morning."

"How old is Annette?" Hoenisch asked.

"Do I have to tell you?"

"No. I assume she's still under 18. Which we don't care about. But I would guess you probably had to have her home early that night."

"I don't think her mother is that picky what time she's got to be home."

"No?"

"I didn't even take her home. I dropped her off at a friend's."

A car drove by the farm and honked. Someone yelled something from the window. Chris twisted around in his seat.

"Oh, oh," he said. "I'm going to get an ass-chewing when I get home."

"Who's that?" Hoenisch asked.

"Ma or dad."

"Should I let you out so you can go talk to them?"

"No. She drove by."

"So," Roddy said. "Do have any idea why somebody would do something like that. Kill those people?"

"No. What I could see of them, I thought—I mean, he seemed real nice, down to earth. I mean, he isn't cocky or—you know—he didn't seem like the type that would screw you over if he got the chance. You know? Seemed real nice. I don't know, you know?"

"Yeah. He doesn't appear to be the type who would hurt anybody," Roddy said.

"Yeah." Chris paused. Sniffed deeply.

"Anything else?" he asked.

Roddy glanced at Hoenisch. He gave the slightest nod.

"Well, I don't know," Hoenisch said.

"We're just trying to figure out what the scoop is here. You know, whoever is involved—it's got to be playing on their mind, you would think. You'd think, inside, it would be bothering them. And I thought by now somebody would have told a friend—or somebody would have talked about those things."

Hoenisch stopped. Chris nodded his head.

"I don't know if you remember this spring—there was an elderly couple killed over in Hamburg," Hoenisch said. "I don't know if you remember hearing about that deal.

"Wendell and I worked on that case. A guy that was involved, that committed those murders, who we talked to a couple of days after the murders, talked about how much pressure you feel inside, how much guilt you feel, and how you get to the point where you just want to unload. After he finally told us what had happened up there, he said he felt 100 percent better because he was finally able to let it out."

Chris pushed his hair out of his eyes.

"I thought by now," Hoenisch said, "somewhere along the line . . ."

"I know I was losing sleep over that car," Chris said. "Christ, I'd see a set of lights come and I'd go tearing ass over there looking out the window thinking it's going to stop."

"Yeah," Hoenisch said. "It wears on you."

Hoenisch pulled out a map of the Kunzes' farm and began explaining to Chris about the tire tracks that were left near the garden. He told him they could tell the order in which the tracks were made. He told him about making plaster casts of the impressions and about going to the crime lab and consulting with experts. He told Chris how they had been able to determine that the front tires were BF Goodrich belted T/A's.

"That's what I got on my car."

"You do?"

"Yeah."

"There aren't many of them around," Hoenisch said. "Very, very few."

"You can get. . . ." Jacobs stopped. He stuffed his hands into the pockets of his coat.

"Oh no, oh no, oh no," he said. He was shaking his head back and forth. "There's no way I'd kill somebody. Oh no. I ain't saying no more till I get a lawyer."

"Yep, well just listen," Hoenisch said. "You don't have to say anything. You just listen to what we say, okay?"

Hoenisch leaned in closer to Chris. He pointed to another track on the map.

"This is the back tire of the car," Hoenisch said. "Want to take a guess at what that is?"

Chris glanced down at the map, then up and out the window. He crossed his arms over his chest. The muscles in his face tightened.

"I don't know," Chris said.

"It's a Duralon DS Premium."

"Uh-hm," Chris said.

"The chances other than your car—I don't think you'll find a car in Central Wisconsin with that on the front. Nobody buys them around here. But the chances of a car other than yours having a BF Goodrich bias tire on the front and a Duralon premium on the back are zero."

"I don't think I like what you're getting at."

"Well, this is what the bottom line is, Chris. We know you've been to the Kunzes' house before."

"Yeah. So?"

"And we know you were back at that house a month before that incident last July."

"I was not," Chris said. "I was not there."

"Helen Kunz told Kenny—Kenny's the one you bought the cars from—that the guy that bought the cars was back and wanted to buy more cars."

"I was not there," Chris said sharply. "I ain't saying no more until I get a lawyer."

"Let me show you something else, Chris." Hoenisch pulled a packet of papers out of his coat.

"Should we get into this?" he asked Roddy.

"It's all right," Roddy said.

"A couple of things first. Number one, we have four search warrants here to cover your parents' house and all their properties.

"Next, right now there is I don't know how many detectives and investigators out in this area contacting virtually every person that we know you know.

"Now, I think you're smart enough to realize what you told us is going to be rather easy as far as checking out. All right? One thing you have going for you right now is cooperation. Okay? Do you understand that?"

"Ah-ha."

"I'll be honest with you," Hoenisch said. "I don't know exactly what happened there. I don't know how many people were involved. We don't have all the evidence back from the Crime Lab as to who did what, but I'll be honest with you—your best shot right now is to get this thing cleared up. Okay?"

"Ah-ha."

"Okay. Are you willing to tell us what the scoop is?"

"I want a lawyer."

"It's up to you. There's going to be a time though—you probably learned this from the last time with the stolen car—now is the time to get this squared away. Okay?"

"Ah-ha."

"This is too big to take the whole blame yourself if you weren't the only one involved."

"I want a lawyer."

"That's fine," Hoenisch said. "We'll get you one. We're not asking you to say anything. We're just trying to get through to you. You're still a young man, Chris, and you got a lot of things to look forward to."

"Listen. Why don't we get going 'cause I want to get ahold of my lawyer."

"All I'm trying to do is work something out for you, okay?" Hoenisch said. "We even got the go-ahead if the logistics of everything is just right, okay? We can probably do something on that stolen car deal for you, okay? That would depend on what the situation is here. Understand what I'm saying . . ."

"I stole the car. So? I had nothing to do with this and I want a lawyer."

"Well, the truth is, you did," Hoenisch said. "And we're going to be able to prove your car was in the garden that night. Now, I'm not saying you killed those people . . ."

"That's why he's giving you the chance," Roddy said. "If you weren't the trigger man, now's the chance to get out of it."

"I want to talk to a lawyer—simple as that."

"Yeah, that's what we're going to be doing."

"Well, let's get going," Chris said. "Can I stop at home first?"

"No," Hoenisch said.

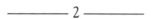

2

The Athens Community Hall/Fire Station, across the street from the funeral home that held the wake for Clarence, Irene, Marie and Randy Kunz, became Command Central as 40 officers from the State Department of Justice, the Marathon and Taylor County sheriff's departments, and the Athens and Medford police departments began rounding up and questioning dozens of Chris's friends.

Among those questioned was Annette Harley, the 17-year-old Chris claimed he "almost got lucky with" the night the Kunzes were murdered.

Annette told investigators that she went to the Medford fireworks with her mother and stayed there with her mother the whole night.

She described Chris as her "steady boyfriend," but said she didn't meet Chris until December.

"December 4th," she said.

"I marked it on my calendar at school."

The media got wind of the round-up and reporters began gathering outside the fire station. Deputies held coats, notebooks and newspapers over the faces of people brought in for questioning. The reporters were told to go away.

"When we have anything of substance, we'll let you know," Lt. Elwood Mason, head of the sheriff's department's detective bureau told them.

"You must be driving the people of Athens crazy," a reporter asked.

"Maybe that's part of the strategy," Mason said.

But if investigators thought that, under enough pressure, someone would talk, they were wrong.

One of the boys who had been with Chris when he purchased a car from the Kunzes told investigators he "did not feel bad about them being killed, seeing as how they lived."

Another—again one of the boys who had been with Chris at the Kunzes' house—said that if Chris had gotten away with murder in July, "then maybe that's why he figured he could get away with stealing a neighbor's car in November."

It was hardly the sort of stuff investigators had anticipated.

By Sunday, John Reid, the state's chief public defender in Wausau, was demanding to see Chris, who was being held at the Marathon County Jail as an alleged party to the crime of murder.

"When I asked to see him, they refused," Reid told a reporter. "The reason I was given was that he already had a lawyer. I asked to confer with the individual himself to see that he had an attorney, but the sergeant said no."

Reid was incensed.

"I've never been turned away from speaking face-to-face with a suspect who has recently been arrested."

At 10:30 p.m. Sunday, after a lengthy meeting with Marathon County District Attorney Rand Krueger, Lt. Mason ordered Chris Jacobs released.

It had been a fiasco, and on Monday, the district attorney met with the media at the courthouse in Wausau.

Two folding banquet tables had been pushed together length-wise, and Krueger sat on the edge of a metal chair placed alone at one end, gripping and ungripping his hands nervously as he answered reporters' questions.

To the out-of-town media, Krueger seemed defensive, almost hostile. Later, the local press would explain that Krueger always seemed defensive and hostile around reporters.

Still, there was something dismissive and unwelcoming—even unpleasant—about his manner. His beard seemed to be an obscuring, rather than a distinguishing, characteristic. His eyes were hidden by a pair of glasses utterly neutral in style. In fact, the only facial feature Krueger displayed with any prominence was his forehead, which was enlarged by a receding hairline and pocked with acne scars.

"There were a lot of things that happened over the weekend, some planned and expected, others, which were the result of executing search warrants and interviews, which were unplanned and unexpected," Krueger said.

"I think there are going to be surprises yet—that's something you always have to allow for. What happened last weekend confirmed what I already believed, at least in a large measure.

"We're not waiting for someone to talk or for a shoe to drop," he said.

"What we are waiting for is a culmination of the events of this past weekend."

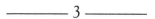

—————— 3 ——————

From a list of items removed from the Jacobses' farmhouse and property on Jan. 29, 1988:

One 1974 two-door Charger (Super B), black with orange stripes on both sides.

Four rounds of live .22-caliber ammunition, recovered from the pocket of Chris Jacobs Jr.—father of Chris Jacobs III—in the kitchen of the Jacobses' Town of Bern home.

One Winchester lever-action rifle, .22-caliber.

One Marlin semi-automatic rifle, .22-caliber.

Fifteen rounds of live .22-caliber ammunition, recovered from a wooden table next to a stereo in Chris Jacobs's bedroom.

Eighty-one spent .22-caliber cartridge casings and two live rounds of .22-caliber ammunition, found in the turntable compartment of the stereo in Chris Jacobs's bedroom.

Twenty spent rounds of .22-caliber ammunition found elsewhere in the stereo system in Chris Jacobs's bedroom.

One spent .22-caliber cartridge casing, found in a cardboard box sitting on the floor of Chris Jacobs's bedroom.

One spent .22-caliber shell casing, found on the floor of Chris Jacobs's bedroom.

One partial box of .22-caliber ammunition, containing 14 live rounds, in Chris Jacobs's bedroom.

One box of .22-caliber ammunition (50 count), found in the master bedroom.

One spent .22-caliber casing found in machine shed.

A yellow ammunition box containing three spent .22-caliber cartridges, found on a window sill in the milk-house.

One *Marshfield Herald* newspaper, dated July 6, 1987, and containing an account of the Kunz family murders.

From a Marathon County Sheriff's Department Report, filed Feb. 19, 1988, by Deputy Michael F. Gaulke:

> When Mr. Kunz and I arrived at the (Kunzes') residence in the Town of Bern, we found that all the doors had been pried open, numerous windows were broken and inside the house, what was left inside the house, was entirely ransacked.
>
> It appeared that someone had gone inside and took whatever was available and threw it around the house, including out the windows.
>
> Speaking of Mr. Kunz, it was difficult to understand exactly what he was concerned with regarding the damage because everything appeared to be very old and discardable.

From a Marathon County Sheriff's Department Report, filed by Detective Roddy:

> On Feb. 24, Germaine Pecher called to report a break-in of a shed at the Clarence Kunz farm.
>
> I contacted Kenneth Kunz by telephone. He advised me that he found an old vise, two kerosene lanterns, one post maul and one red tool box containing tools, missing from the garage. He advised that a lot of items were thrown around.

One item Roddy and Hoenisch had expected to find during their search of the Jacobses' property was a Remington Nylon .22-caliber semi-automatic rifle.

Several of Chris's friends had told authorities that he owned the gun, and Judy Jacobs said she remembered buying the weapon, but didn't know where it was.

"Haven't seen it in years," she said.

Chris's father, Chris Jacobs, Jr., said he used to keep the weapon in the ceiling joist of the garage, using it on occasion to shoot skunks.

The rifle had a plastic stock and forearm, and the two detectives decided to take a drive out to the Kunzes' house and make a careful search of the Kunzes' kitchen floor. After all, Randy had received a pretty sharp blow to the head. If the Remington Nylon had been used, perhaps some of its plastic pieces broke off.

The two crawled around on their hands and knees for almost an hour. Some of the appliances had been moved out, and the kitchen seemed much bigger than Hoenisch remembered.

"Ah! Look at this," Hoenisch said.

"Plastic?" Roddy asked.

"Not exactly. Take a look."

Roddy bent down beside Hoenisch. There, where the refrigerator used to be in the northeast corner of the kitchen, wedged between some cracks in the tile surface and jammed against the wall, was a .22-caliber casing.

In early March, with Chris serving a 60-day work-release sentence at the Taylor County Jail, Rand Krueger convened a John Doe investigation into the Kunz murders.

A small courtroom was set aside for the proceedings. The window blinds were drawn. Paper covered the door's window. For the better part of a day, many of people questioned during the January blitz were brought to the Marathon County Courthouse, where they were questioned under oath.

One of the stars of the John Doe was Wayne Weiler, one of Chris's best friends.

Wayne told authorities that one night, about a year after Chris had bought the cars from the Kunzes, he and Chris were driving around when they passed the Kunzes' house.

According to Wayne, Chris told him that when he was in the house he had seen a fat wad of $100 bills in the drawer of a file cabinet.

For weeks, Wayne said, Chris talked about how he wanted to go back and get the money. Wayne said he thought Chris was trying to get him to go with him.

Judy Jacobs also testified.

Krueger asked her whether or not Chris had visited the Kunzes' house in the months preceding the murders.

"What he told me," Judy said, "is that he had stopped there to look at a car, that he had talked to—he called her an old lady, an elderly lady. He said he never went back about it. I didn't ask him why or anything."

A few days later, on a Friday, the Marathon County Sheriff's Department, hinting that the John Doe had uncovered important new information, took the extraordinary step of calling a news conference to announce that on the following Monday it would be digging for evidence in the Kunz murders.

Reporters were invited to watch the excavation, and would be escorted to the site by deputies.

From a Marathon County Sheriff's Department report filed by Deputy Alan Phillips:

On March 11, at about 8:30 a.m., I was listening in on a press conference at the Marathon County Sheriff's office.

While standing outside of the door with other members of the sheriff's department, I recognized a person I knew was associated with the state Public Defender's office. He also apparently was listening in on the press conference. After about five or 10 minutes, I left the sheriff's department.

I was in my car and ready to leave when the public defender's representative knocked on my window.

I rolled my window down and the representative identified himself as Weldon Nelson. Nelson advised me that he was indeed with the public defender's office.

Nelson then proceeded to ask me if I had attended the John Doe hearing held earlier in the week. As I was telling Nelson that I had better not say anything, Nelson opened his wallet and began removing his card.

Nelson told me that if I just wanted to "talk," I should contact him.

I then told Nelson that I felt he did not realize who I was. I then showed Nelson my sheriff's department identification and Nelson folded up his wallet, turned and walked away without saying another word.

Monday could not have been less ideal: A weekend storm had left six inches of snow on the ground, and the morning was grey, cold and windy.

The half-acre site, about 25 miles west of the Kunz home, had once been the site of an old barn and manure pit. Chris—who, together with his father, ran a part-time excavating business—had been hired over the summer to level the barn and push it into the manure pit.

A witness told police that Chris had accomplished the task in the driving rain. He said he couldn't understand what Chris was doing out there.

"He wasn't even wearing a hat," the witness said.

The date, he said, was July 5.

Investigators figured that if Chris buried the remains of the Fabers' car, perhaps he buried Helen, or the murder weapon, or some other evidence, in the manure pit. They planned to use a bulldozer and a backhoe to dig a pit 50 feet wide, 100 feet long, and 10 feet deep.

Every shovel of cow shit and barn rubble would be sifted through and examined. It would be a stinking, cold, miserable task.

"Like looking for a needle in a septic tank," is the way one detective put it.

Five detectives—including, of course, Roddy and Hoenisch—were assigned to the dig. An officer from the state Department of Criminal Investigation was on hand, as well as a forensic anthropologist.

By noon, so were virtually all the major media outlets in the state. About 40 reporters showed up. Cars. Vans. Trucks with transmitters mounted on the their tops. A television crew hovered overhead in a helicopter.

One reporter compared it to Geraldo Rivera's "The Mystery of Al Capone's Vault."

Neighbors came, bringing snacks and thermoses of hot coffee. Spectators drove in from out of town. Mothers came with their babies wrapped in blankets, their children bundled in snow suits. Elderly people sat in their cars and watched, their engines on, their heaters running.

Two den mothers brought nine members of the Owen-Withee Cub Scout Den 4, Pack 519.

"So they can view law enforcement in action," one of the women said.

Helen Kunz had become perhaps the most famous missing person in Wisconsin history, and just about everyone was hoping to be there when her legendary remains were uncovered.

But not everyone.

Around 2 p.m., a silver Volvo arrived and Kenny Kunz climbed out of the back seat. A sheriff's deputy had called in the morning to see if he wanted to come out, and he declined. In the early afternoon, he changed his mind, and some friends gave him a ride out.

"I just want to know what happened to my mother," he said.

He stood at the cusp of the pit, a cap with ear-flaps pulled low over his eyes, clutching a cup of coffee, watching Hoenisch, calf-deep in sludge, his brown sheriff's department cover-alls splattered with mud, poke through mounds of manure.

He began to cry.

The dig began in the southeast corner of the property and worked its way west. By dusk, excavators had covered about a third of the pit and had found nothing.

Everyone was back bright and early on Tuesday.

At noon, the forensic anthropologist said he had to attend to some other commitments.

"Give me a call if you find something," he said.

By dusk, investigators had still found nothing.

Digging continued from 8 a.m. to 5 p.m. Wednesday. Nothing. Another fiasco?

"At least we know we can eliminate this site," Lt. Elwood Mason said.

Chapter 3

The Big Thaw

—— 1 ——

It was like one of those hidden-picture drawings that you sometimes find in a child's magazine: A cat is hidden in a billowing cloud, a typewriter is hidden in the leaves of a tree, a camel is hidden in a woman's hair.

Then, you see it.

And then forever you cannot help but see it, and you can't believe you didn't see it before.

For Roddy, it was a small tree, broken off about eight feet from the ground. Beside it, a crust of ice over the swampy earth. There was a sound—water. The creek nearby. Swollen by snow-melt. There was a smell. Clean. The smell of thawing woods. A movement. Birds.

And then. Then a piece of blue. Blue clothing. Pants. Pants under the thinning ice.

A guard was posted and Roddy waited for Ray Matejczyk and Steve Harrington, analysts from the State Crime Lab, to come up from Madison. They would be there the next day—March 31.

171

The remains had been found very near the spot where Daniel and Patrick Harding had encountered that awful smell while fishing on the Big Rib River in July.

Roddy himself had visited the area in July, after another fisherman called the police and said something in the area smelled like a dead animal. He had found nothing then, but when Chris became a suspect, he decided to return to the area in the spring.

The spot was a marsh just off County Highway M, less than five miles from the Jacobs' Town of Goodrich farm. The spot was less than four miles west of a creek into which Chris had thrown some of the parts stripped from Faber's car. That spot also was just off Highway M.

A few miles further east, in a swampy area also off Highway M, a hunter had found two chrome rims on the bottom of a creek. The rims belonged to Alan Hopperdietzell, an Athens resident who had reported them stolen in April 1987.

Chris's friend, Wayne Weiler, had told a police informant in November that Chris allegedly had been involved in the theft. Chris was never charged in the matter, but it was on the basis of that tip that Marathon County authorities joined Taylor County authorities in their November 10 search of the Jacobses' Town of Goodrich property.

The water froze overnight, and when Roddy returned to the site in the morning, he could stand on the road and see a little portion of the blue clothing sticking up above the ice.

Matejczyk and Harrington arrived a little after 8:30 a.m., and Roddy led them over a partially submerged log to the remains. While Matejczyk shot pictures and video, Harrington hopped over to a piece of high ground near the broken tree and began to remove shards of ice, revealing a pair of pants, some bones, a sweater, all submerged in about two feet of water.

Roddy and Detective Sergeant Harold Bean held a sheet, while Harrington and Detective Phil Johnson lifted the lower portion of the remains out of the water. The men worked for about an hour, then Roddy said he better go tell Kenny and Germaine.

Kenny was taking a driver's test and couldn't be located, so Roddy returned with Germaine.

"There's mostly just bones left," Roddy told her as they drove north into Taylor County. She shook her head, overwhelmed and unable to speak.

At the swamp, Germaine waited in the car while Roddy checked on the status of the recovery. After a few minutes, he opened her door and squatted down beside her.

"Germaine," he said. "This will be hard. But, I would like you to look at the clothes and tell us if you think they belong to Helen."

And so Germaine was brought to the Crime Lab van, and there, in the late afternoon of an early spring day, the sheet was opened and Germaine leaned against Roddy and shook—all her body shook—as she forced her eyes to remain open, as she forced her eyes to see.

The blue pants and black and white tennis shoes looked like Helen's, she said. The red socks looked like the ones Helen liked to wear. But the blouse—Helen had been wearing a blue and white flowered blouse. Algae had turned the blue flowers green. The sweater looked like Helen's, but Helen's sweater was yellow. Algae had turned the sweater green as well.

"Here," Germaine said. "Let me look at the hem of the pants."

Roddy turned the hem inside out. It was pinned with safety pins.

"Yes, Helen's," Germaine said. "Helen would pin them until I had time to hem them properly. "These are Helen's clothes.

"All that's left."

From autopsy report W88–114:

This is Dr. (Robert) Huntington on Good Friday, 1 April 88.

In a small bag, neatly stapled and labeled as "3–31–88, 3:25 p.m., jaw plus other bones," is identified one humerus, two vertebrae and a mandible. The mandible has not had molar teeth in it for a long while and the only teeth in fact now present are incisors and right cuspid. Extensive wear and probable bad periodontal disease is shown.

At 1:12 p.m. I remove the lead tag from the body bag. Attention is immediately directed in this body bag to the skull, which is in a separate plastic bag along with some leaf debris. From this leaf debris is removed a strong suspect for a small caliber leaden cartridge. This was identified first per X-ray—it was not in the head itself.

A study of the skull itself shows a fairly small skull with a ½-by-½-inch penetration hole in the mid-forehead at a level about 1 inch to 1¼ inch above the nasion. The flare of this hole is with the outer table wounding wider, and this is therefore interpreted as an exit wound.

The question of where the entry for this exit would be results in study of the remaining skull, and we can show that top and bottom of the right orbit are badly smashed through and largely missing and extensive fractures radiate from the region.

The hypothesis is that then the round entered from below right maxilla without hitting mandible and proceeded cephalad.

In the left side of the blouse are four possible cut wounds. The inner undershirt-type garment is exceedingly ragged and might have corresponding holes, but there are so many holes, it's hard to be sure.

From a report filed by Division of Criminal Investigation Special Agent Richard F. Berghammer concerning autopsy W88–114:

> The skeletal remains were in a black body bag with some tissue remaining on the joints and in the pelvic area as well as decomposed tissue floating in the lower part of the body bag.
>
> Drs. Huntington, (Ken) Bennett and (Donald) Simley determined that this was a female, elderly, with some arthritis. Measurements were taken by Dr. Bennett, and he estimated the femur bone would indicate that the female was possibly 4 feet 11½ inches to 5 feet tall.
>
> There was a hole in the forehead which appeared to have been a bullet wound. Located in the body bag with the skull was one lead round.
>
> It appeared from the bullet hole that the bullet may have entered from the bottom of the right orbit and entered the skull from below, then exiting the forehead.

From a letter to Sheriff LeRoy Schillinger from Dr. Donald Simley, forensic dentist:

On April 1, 1988, at the request of the State Crime Laboratory, I attended an autopsy on the decomposed and essentially skeletonized remains of an individual recovered in Taylor County. I took the skull of this individual back to my office to complete an examination and a dental charting.

It is my opinion that to within a reasonable degree of dental certainty, the remains that I examined, clinically and radiographically, on April 1 are those of Helen Kunz.

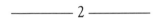

——— 2 ———

The tests conducted by the State Crime Laboratory in Madison on weapons and bullet casings collected during the investigation brought mixed, but promising, results.

In all, 18 guns seized from the Jacobs family and from friends of Chris Jacobs were turned over to the Crime Lab for testing, along with nine .22-caliber spent casings found in the Kunz home.

The crime lab concluded that none of the guns had fired the spent casings.

However, the Crime Lab concluded that 29 of the 101 bullet casings removed by investigators from Chris Jacob's bedroom were fired from the same weapon that fired the nine bullet casings found in the Kunz home.

"Bingo," Roddy said.

Furthermore, the Crime Lab concluded, based on ejector and rifling characteristics observed on the matched casings from the Kunz and Jacobs homes, the bullets were probably fired from a rifle manufactured by Remington.

And while the technicians couldn't be sure, they said that if they had to pick one weapon, they would look for a Remington Nylon 66.

The sheriff's department began keeping Chris under constant surveillance, and made no effort to conceal its activities. Deputies kept detailed records. Here is a typical day, gleaned from a sheriff's department investigative report:

7:26 a.m.—Chris Jacobs III leaves Taylor County Jail in a green and white Dodge pickup. Detective Krueger and Detective Fussell will be following him all day. He left jail and we immediately lost him as he did some jogging around the streets of Medford.

When we located him again, he was at a car parts store in the parking lot talking to a male subject.

7:45 a.m.—Chris pulled over on a side road and got out of his vehicle.

Detective Fussell and I both passed him as he watched us drive by, then I continued on and Detective Fussell pulled over to the side of the road. Chris came out of the side road, pulled up behind Fussell and talked to him and asked if he was following him.

They then proceeded and I pulled off on a side road to let both of them go by. Chris turned on the same road I was on and pulled up in front of me and got out of his vehicle, and I got out of mine.

He said, "I suppose you're not following me either."

I said, "It's a public highway."

Chris was talking about how this was a bunch of bullshit and we better not be loitering around his farm and various comments as such.

To each of his remarks, I simply stated that it was a public highway.

Chris said it must not be a public highway if he gets chased off a public road and is told not to loiter near our van.

I did not know which van he was referring to, but he has stopped at the stakeout truck near the north farm and that may be what he's talking about.

7:54 a.m.—Chris Jacobs arrives at his parents' residence.

8 a.m.—The green and white pickup comes out of the yard and towards where we are parked. As I approached the truck, we could see that it was Chris Jr. and Mrs. Jacobs, not Chris III.

They slowed down and waved at me. I continued on. The truck then turned around and went back to the residence.

11:19 a.m.—About 30 to 40 minutes ago, Chris drove the green and white pickup to the north farm and a green Ford LTD followed him. We followed.

Chris was standing in the milk-house door watching me drive by. An older, heavy-set gentleman was standing in the road by the green LTD. He had a stainless steel hook on his left hand—a prosthetic device. He did not try to stop me as I drove by. Just waved.

I called the office on the TAC channel. They advised me that we had been spotted in our surveillance.

Of course, we were already very much aware of that fact.

11:46 a.m.—Green and white pickup and a tractor with manure spreader are leaving the north farm. The green Ford LTD is also leaving. We will follow.

12:05 p.m.—Green and white pickup return to farm, but the green Ford LTD continues on. It turns east on Highway F, so we will not have to contend with the Ford LTD for a while.

12:13 p.m.—Fussell and I met on Weiler Road, about ½ mile south of the Jacobs' residence. A green Ford LTD pulled up.

The gentleman with a hook for a left hand was very excited. Vehement. Irate. He accused us of following him.

When I tried to explain that we were not following him, he would not listen to reason. He said he didn't do anything wrong and he wanted it stopped. I told him I didn't know who he was and we were not following him.

His passenger took down our license numbers and they departed.

4:15 p.m.—The green and white pickup left the Jacobs residence. I was unable to see who was the driver. Appeared to be only one person in the vehicle.

I notified Fussell that I was leaving my spot and he should stay there. By the time I got about ½ mile up the road, the vehicle was nowhere in sight.

Not sure if it was Chris or his dad or if they were just playing games.

Finally located green and white pickup parked behind a residence. By the time I had turned around, the vehicle was already returning home. Fussell said it appeared that the person that got out of the truck was Chris Jr., not Chris III.

7:05 p.m.—Two vehicles pulled out of yard and headed east. One is a van, unable to tell what the other was. Fussell asked if the headlights coming down the road were Chris's. I told him I wasn't sure.

7:25 p.m.—I contacted Taylor County Sheriff's office on the point-to-point radio to check to see if Chris had returned from work. They advised he had. His mother dropped him off.

Apparently, one of the two vehicles that went east contained Chris. We lost him again.

Shortly after Helen's body was found, Judy Jacobs began contacting law enforcement officials, insisting that her son had not been involved in the Kunz murders and that someone was trying to frame him.

During one telephone call, she told Taylor County Deputy Norm Dassow that she was afraid Marathon County deputies would plant some of the shell casings taken from Chris's room at the murder scene.

She gave him the names of people Chris knew and suggested one of them might have stolen the Remington rifle authorities were searching for.

In another conversation, she told Dassow that she had been over Chris's alibi time and time again, and that each time, Chris insisted he had been alone that night.

She said her son was growing depressed. He was spending a lot of time sitting alone, drinking.

One Saturday morning, Roddy was at home when the phone rang. It was Judy.

She wanted to know if Roddy had checked out the list of names she had given Dassow. She wanted to know what the neighbors had been saying about Chris. She wanted to know about the tire tracks.

"You know, Judy," Roddy told her. "I've got four children of my own. I've got 10 grandchildren. If any of my children were suspects in a crime, I'd want to know the truth."

"Yes, yes," she said.

"I would want to know, Judy, because if any of my children were involved in something of this nature—something like the murder of five people—I would want to know because that child needs some kind of professional help.

"See what I'm saying. I would want that child to get professional help. I would want to know for the rest of my family's safety. And for the safety of my neighbors."

"My son is innocent," Judy told him.

July 5, 1988.

A year had passed since the murders, and reporters filed their obligatory one-year-later stories, most pinning their pieces on interviews with Rand Krueger, who had announced he would not seek another term as Marathon County's district attorney.

"It's like a huge jigsaw puzzle," Krueger told Mary Jo Kewley of *The Wausau Daily Herald*.

"Only it's a huge jigsaw puzzle in which we haven't seen the cover of the box."

Krueger repeated the metaphor with Peter Maller of the *Milwaukee Sentinel*.

"Usually, when you start a jigsaw puzzle, you start with the border," he said. "In this case, I'd say we have 90% of the border and we have some chunks of the middle.

"We definitely have more pieces in our possession now than there were in the winter."

Actually, a crucial portion of the puzzle had fallen apart.

Roddy and Hoenisch had taken the plaster casts of the tire impressions made in the Kunzes' garden to the B.F. Goodrich Tire Co. headquarters in Akron, Ohio.

There they met with several design engineers who told them that they were absolutely certain that the B.F. Goodrich tires on Chris Jacobs's car did not match the tracks found in the Kunzes' garden.

The BF Goodrich belted T/A tires that made the tracks at the Kunzes' garden were indeed in the 70 series, just as Roddy had concluded back in January.

Unfortunately, the tires on the front of Chris's car were the larger 60 series. No match.

"Well, it's obvious what happened," Roddy said.

"When Chris bought his tires, he had the narrower 70 series tires put on the front and the wider 60 series put on the back.

"Then, sometime before July 4, 1987, he takes the 60s off the back and replaces them with the Duralons. The 70s stay on the front, and that's what's on the car when he drives it into the garden.

"So, then sometime between July and when we seized the car in January, Chris takes the 70 series off the front and replaces them with the 60 series."

"Which means," Hoenisch said, "that—if we're lucky—the 70 series are still laying around the Jacobses' yard somewhere."

Oh, God, it was hot.

Hot and dusty.

No rain for weeks. Temperatures in the 90s. Corn withered. Cattle sulked. The ground cracked open like a neglected wound.

It was the second summer of drought; everyone was hurting, but small dairy operations, such as the Jacobs farm, hurt worse.

Experts estimated that Wisconsin's corn crop would be 25% to 50% less than anticipated. Altogether, crop loss could exceed 70%.

Farmers with lower milk production were not going to have enough cash to pay for the feed the drought kept them from growing.

The Wisconsin Bankers Association was told that as many as 15% of its farm loan customers would be driven out of business.

It was not much later than 1 p.m. when Hoenisch, together with three other detectives, showed up at the Jacobses' Town of Bern farm with a search warrant authorizing them to seize two BF Goodrich belted T/A tires, series 70.

Chris III and Chris Jr. were cutting hay across the road, but Judy Jacobs was there, and the four detectives began to look around. A few minutes later, Chris Jr. pulled his tractor into the driveway.

"Get that goddamn squad car out of the way or I'm going to run it over," he yelled. Hoenisch could hardly hear him above the tractor's engine.

"Get that goddamn car out of the way!"

"Okay, okay," Hoenisch yelled back. It was Sergeant Harold Bean's squad. Hoenisch didn't realize it, but the keys were in the ignition. As Hoenisch was about to get Bean from the barn, Chris III jumped off the back of the tractor, ran to Bean's car and opened the door.

"Chris," Hoenisch yelled. "Stay the hell out of that car. Close the door, or you'll be arrested."

Chris III got into the car, locked the door and drove it through the yard and into a neighboring field. He then got out, slammed the door shut and walked back into the yard.

Hoenisch told him he was under arrest.

"In that case," he said, and threw Bean's car keys into the field.

From a Marathon County Sheriff's Department report filed by Detective Hoenisch:

> Chris III was eventually taken to jail.
>
> We then continued our search. During the entire search, Chris Jr. followed us around, hollering and shouting. At one point, he told me he believes I killed the Kunz family and I'm trying to cover it up by blaming his son.

He also accused Detective Wendell Roddy of being in-volved in the Kunz murders with me. He also claimed he has information that indicates that District Attorney Rand Krueger may also have been involved in the Kunz murders because he heard he was "stoned out of his mind" in the Athens area July 4.

Chris Jr. also accused me of stealing $400 in cash that he had in his house the last time a search warrant was issued in January. He also accused me of stealing a $4,000 coin collection.

At one point, he walked up to me and said that if I liked to dig around in shit so much, maybe I'd like to dig around "up his ass" for a while.

He also told me he'd like to get me in a ring sometime when I'm off duty and go at it with boxing gloves on or "bare knuckles," whichever way I'd like it.

At one point, Mr. Jacobs hollered at Detective Schroeder, who was videotaping parts of the search, and told him that if he didn't stop taking pictures, he'd shove the camera up his ass.

The aforementioned comments are only a sampling of the verbal abuse officers were subjected to while executing the search warrant.

Unpleasant, but Hoenisch found what he came for. The two tires were sent to the state Crime Lab.

Chris was held through the weekend at the County Jail, and on Monday, July 11, he was charged with one count of obstructing a police officer and one misdemeanor count of operating an auto without the owner's consent.

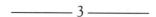

———— 3 ————

To obtain a conviction, Krueger needed to go to court and show not just that a car with tires like those belonging to Chris Jacobs had been in the Kunzes' garden the night of the murders. It was essential that he show that Chris's very tires made the tracks.

Without that link, there could be no chance of conviction.

"A positive tire identification," Krueger said, "would form the linchpin of the case."

The state Crime Lab studied the tires. It studied the tracks. And then it concluded, much to everyone's dismay, that it could not make a positive match.

The sheriff's department brought in Peter McDonald, the former manager of Tire Design at the Firestone Tire & Rubber Co. in Akron, Ohio.

McDonald, who with his bald pate and white mustache resembled the cartoon millionaire in the board game Monopoly, left Firestone after 28 years to establish Tire Footprint Identification, an Ohio-based tire forensics consulting firm.

His effectiveness was legendary.

In 1976, while still with Firestone, he helped solve the murder of two prostitutes in Monterey, California, by identifying the tires on the killer's car using a police picture of tire prints found at the crime scene.

His examination of a single tread mark in Nottingham, Pennsylvania, cleared a prime suspect and pointed police toward the true killer.

Stories about McDonald had appeared in *Time* and *People* magazines. In the *People* article, he is pictured standing in a pile of tires dressed like Sherlock Holmes: meerschaum pipe, spy-glass, deerstalker cap.

"He has created bookends out of tire models, oil paintings from photos of tire particles enlarged 50,000 times, and even a five-foot-high stained-glass window in a pattern based on a tire print," the *People* story says.

"A show of his artwork is touring Ohio."

From a Marathon County Sheriff's Department report:

> His recent claim to fame was to appear in a trivia game, on a card that reads, "Peter McDonald helps police 'track' killers using what method?"

183

The answer is, "Matching tire tracks."

In August, McDonald spent four days at the state Crime Lab in Madison. On the left rear tire, a Duralon, he found a stone caught in the tread and a nearby surface abrasion that matched a track left in the garden.

His opinion, which he would repeat in court: "No other tire in the world could have made that imprint."

The Crime Lab analyst Steven Harrington was asked to take another look at the tires and review McDonald's work. Harrington concluded that the left rear tire was consistent with the tire imprint, but he could not make a positive identification.

Now there was the risk that a skilled defense attorney could pit expert against expert, undermining the probative value of the tire evidence.

The materials were shipped off to the FBI laboratory in Washington, where they were examined by analyst William Bodziak.

Bodziak's results: He, too, could not be positive that the left rear tire matched the impression. It was, however, consistent.

But on one of the BF Goodrich tires recovered from the Jacobs farm, he found a cut that matched a track left in the garden.

A positive match.

From a Marathon County Sheriff's Department report, filed by Detective Randy Hoenisch:

On Tuesday, August 30, 1988, an arrest warrant was issued by Circuit Judge Vincent Howard charging Chris J. Jacobs III with five counts of being party to the crime of first degree murder.

Because of problems encountered by law enforcement in the past at the Jacobs residence, it was decided that the Jacobs residence would be kept under surveillance until it could be determined that Chris Jacobs III was on the property, at which time an arrest team utilizing members of the Special Response team would effect the arrest, preferably in the early morning hours of Wednesday, August 31.

From the front page of *The Wausau Daily Herald* Aug. 30, 1988:

Is Kunz investigation near end?

The Marathon County Sheriff's Department's pledge to finish the Kunz investigation by the first week in September was "wishful thinking," said Marathon County District Attorney Rand Krueger.

Lt. Elwood Mason, who heads the detective bureau, recently said that the investigation would be complete by the last week in August or the first week in September, after a forensic investigator who specializes in tire prints studied evidence.

"He is entitled to his opinion," Krueger said.

Continuing the Marathon County Sheriff's Department report filed by Detective Randy Hoenisch:

At approximately 3:30 a.m. Wednesday, August 31, Deputy Mark Wanta and I took a position in a corn field approximately ⅛ of a mile west of the Jacobs residence.

At approximately 7:22 a.m., Chris Jacobs III was observed walking from his house to the barn on the property. The arrest team was notified and responded to the Jacobs property.

At approximately 7:25 a.m., Chris Jacobs III was taken into custody and arrested without incident.

I read the original arrest warrant to Chris Jacobs III and showed him the judge's signature on the original warrant. Detective Roddy and I then transported Chris Jacobs III to the Marathon County Jail.

Chapter 4

The Trial

──── 1 ────

Because of intense pretrial publicity, a pool of 120 potential jurors was assembled across the state in Green Bay. From that group of 120, a panel of 26 would be selected.

Then the prosecution and defense teams—consisting of Special Prosecutor Rand Krueger for the state and court-appointed lawyers John Reid and Weldon Nelson for the defense—would each be allowed to dismiss six, leaving 14 jurors, including two alternates, to hear the case.

Jury selection began on October 2, 1989—a Monday—and continued for three days.

Before selection began, Nelson introduced Chris to the potential jurors. Chris wore a slate-grey, faintly striped suit, a white shirt, a blue tie. His hair was trimmed, spritzed and combed. He looked like the president of the campus Young Republicans Club.

"Good morning," he said. Soft. Shy. "Nice to meet you all."

Jurors nodded. Several smiled. One woman slightly lifted her hand from her lap and gave a small wave.

Jury selection lasted nine hours on Monday, 11 hours on Tuesday, 15 hours on Wednesday, ending just before midnight.

Nine women. Five men. A baker. A farmer. A supper club owner. A homemaker. A student. A retired truck driver. A retired teacher. A retired meter reader.

Deputies escorted them home so they could pack, then they were placed on a bus, told to kiss their spouses from a distance, and taken to Marathon County, where they would remain sequestered until the end of the trial.

Krueger's opening remarks were lengthy and they were complicated and they were technical—just as the trial itself would be—but they were delivered in a cogent, well-organized fashion. The discomforting edginess Krueger had displayed to journalists during his news conferences was gone. He seemed perfectly at ease.

His beard clipped short, his grey hair swept back, he appeared distinguished, even elegant.

Krueger began by introducing Roddy and Hoenisch, who, he explained, had been the case's key investigators and would remain seated beside him at the counsel table for the course of the trial.

Roddy and Hoenisch smiled stiffly. It was Sergeant Hoenisch now. The detective had been promoted in January.

The state's case, Krueger warned the jury, would be based on circumstantial, rather than direct, evidence.

"I guess I would define direct evidence as being the kind of evidence that is based upon eyewitness testimony. This homicide case does not include eyewitness testimony. Most homicide cases do not.

"Most murders are not committed in front of witnesses.

"Consequently, this case, like many cases, calls or requires us to in large measure base our case on circumstantial evidence.

"I am sure that most of you are familiar at least in a general way with Sherlock Holmes. As you may recall, what Sherlock Holmes did was discover a number of other facts, and then based upon the facts he had at hand, the facts that he knew, he was able to deduce other facts.

"That's what circumstantial evidence is all about."

Krueger used fingerprints as an example: A fingerprint provides circumstantial evidence that a person was at the place where a fingerprint was found.

It was a calculated example. Krueger's case would rest on the vehicular equivalent to fingerprints—tire tracks—to prove Chris had been to the Kunzes' house the night of the murders.

"Another illustration," Krueger said. "I had the occasion recently to be out at my sister's farm, and in walking in the woods I saw evidence of deer—hoof prints and the remains of deer presence—around an apple tree.

"Obviously from seeing the hoof prints and from seeing the other evidence of the deer, I could conclude—I could deduce—that deer had been there, although I did not see them."

Another calculated example. The tire tracks would be like hoof prints, the deer feces would be like the shell casings.

"There are some things in this case we can't prove," Krueger said.

"We don't have a murder weapon. The defendant is charged as a party to the crime, which means I think in layman's terms that he participated in these murders.

"But I can't prove who pulled the trigger," Krueger told them. "I can't prove who participated with the defendant."

Krueger knew that Chris's defense would focus the jury on the Kunzes' lifestyle, and he attempted to defuse the issue.

"To some extent, this trial is the story of the Kunz family," he said.

"The Kunz family was different. I want to say unique, but that may not do them justice. They lived alone in a situation that I think probably only can be described as maybe turn-of-the-century rustic.

"There was no running water in the house. They had electricity and telephone. Frankly, the place was a mess. Maybe you can can even go so far as to describe it as filthy.

"Judging from the money that was found in the house, they didn't have to live that way, but they did."

Krueger told them about Kenny's drinking problem. The pornography. The seclusion.

"I tell you this now because the Kunz family is not the Nelson family. This is not 'Ozzie and Harriet.' This is not 'Father Knows Best.' This is not 'Leave it to Beaver.'

"These are people you probably wouldn't choose as friends. Indeed, they are people who didn't choose many friends, didn't have many friends, and in part that's what formed the real conundrum, the real mystery for the Sheriff's Department in investigating this case because the number of people who even knew that these people existed was extremely limited.

"They kept to themselves.

"They didn't bother anybody."

Krueger then moved to the heart of his case.

First, motive.

"One of the things that always springs to mind—not only in the minds of law enforcement, but in the minds of anybody who thinks about crimes like this—is motive," Krueger told the jurors.

"Motive is the reason why things happen, why people do things. We like to think that there are motives for this kind of carnage."

"Over $20,000 in cash was found in the house," Krueger said. "I think robbery was the motive for these homicides."

A witness, he said, would testify that Chris had told him the Kunzes had a lot of cash in their house, and that he wanted to go back and get it.

Second, the shell casings.

Experts, Krueger told them, would testify that all five victims were shot with .22-caliber bullets. Irene, at least twice, likely three times, in the back of the head. Clarence, twice in the face. Marie, once in the head. Randy, three times, once in the arm and twice in the head. Helen, once in the head.

Nine .22-caliber shell casings were found at the murder scene. All had been fired from the same .22-caliber rifle, one that had probably been manufactured by Remington. ,

Twenty-nine shell casings removed from Chris Jacobs's bedroom had been fired from the same rifle that had fired the spent shells found at the Kunz home.

A .22-caliber Remington Nylon 66 rifle purchased by Chris's mother in the late 1970s has never been recovered.

Third, the tire tracks.

Experts would testify that sometime after 9:30 p.m. July 4 and before 4:30 a.m. July 5, someone parked a car beside the Kunzes' garden. Randy's car was then driven into the garden and parked. The intruder's car then left.

The intruder's car left tracks. Those tracks positively match a tire on Chris Jacobs's car and a tire found in Chris Jacobs's yard several months after the slayings.

Fourth, Chris's alibi.

Chris told investigators he spent most of the night of July 4 with his girlfriend, Annette Harley. Annette would testify that she did not meet Chris until five months later.

"I anticipate calling at least one, if not both, of the defendant's parents to testify. It goes without saying that they will not be eager to testify for the state.

"I believe that the defendant's mother will testify that she and her husband really don't know where their son was in the late evening hours and early morning hours of July 4 and 5.

"I believe that she will also testify and the evidence will show that later he told her that he had gone to the fireworks in Medford and then had gone to another farm property and, alone, had parked his car in the driveway and sat there and drank some beer at some time after the fireworks and before he went home on that fateful evening.

"If that is what he did, it's impossible to check out."

Krueger then closed:

"I believe that the evidence will show that what happened on the fourth and fifth of July 1987 is that the defendant, along with at least one other, was at the Kunz residence. That he, along with at least one other, drove to and parked his car in the garden area. That the motive for his being there was to get the money that he knew the Kunzes had.

"I believe the evidence will show that Marie Kunz was the first to die. I believe the evidence will show that Irene and Clarence were killed in a state of repose or sleep.

"It's consistent with the evidence in the case to suggest that Randy and Helen came home from the fireworks and confronted the intruders, and that in a struggle, Randy Kunz was killed in the kitchen of the house.

"It's consistent with the evidence and I believe that the evidence will show that Helen Kunz was abducted in Randy's car and that's how it got up to the garden, and that later she was removed in the suspect vehicle and taken north to Taylor County where she was killed."

Krueger thanked the jury and sat down.

Krueger had begun his remarks just after 10:30 a.m. It was now 2:35 p.m.

The courtroom was quiet. The ceiling fans whirled. A reporter dropped his notebook and retrieved it from the floor. Chris scooted his chair in a tad. Someone coughed.

Public Defender Weldon Nelson looked up at Circuit Judge Vincent K. Howard and requested a break.

Krueger's opening remarks were a lecture in physics, a class in logic and deductive reason. Dull, perhaps. But his was a case built on science.

Weldon Nelson's opening remarks, which began, "We are gathered here now with a serious and difficult task in front of us," were a sermon on Sunday, a rally before the big game. Visceral, they sought to create reasonable doubt by generating revulsion and suspicion.

"Now let me tell you something about what I expect the evidence to show," he said.

"The Kunzes were a family that lived like people lived in maybe the 1930s. The house they lived in lacked indoor plumbing. Their meals were cooked on a wood-burning stove.

"But they did have a color television and a VCR. And what did they watch on their VCR? This family that included an 80-year-old, 70-year-olds, one 50-year-old and a 30-year-old watched X-rated videotapes that they bought by mail order. They answered mail order ads for these movies from among the many pornographic magazines that they had in the house.

"They hoarded the money that the most elderly family members got from their Social Security checks. Of the six members of the family, only Kenneth had employment.

"We expect the evidence to show that incest pervaded this family.

"We expect the testimony will be that Helen Kunz was or may have been the mother of Kenneth Kunz, and that her brother, Clarence, was or may have been Kenneth's father.

"We expect the testimony from Kenneth Kunz will be that Randy Kunz and Helen Kunz slept in the same bed.

"We expect the testimony will be that about three weeks prior to July 4th, Helen Kunz was in Weiler's Hardware Store in nearby Athens where she did two things.

"One, she bought a box of .22-caliber bullets, and two, she remarked to the owner that all her family did was sit around and watch dirty movies and that she was so mad she could kill them all.

"Even though she bought .22-caliber shells, the evidence will show that no weapon capable of firing .22-caliber ammunition was found in the Kunz house.

"We would have preferred to let the Kunz family secret remain secret. We had no desire to sully their memories. We agree that what happened to the Kunz family was certainly a tragedy—no matter what kind of people they were. No matter what they were like, they did not deserve to die like they did."

"But we have no choice but to bring these matters to your attention.

"For the question here is what did happen to the Kunzes. We believe you must know everything in order to fairly decide. If we did not raise these issues, we would be risking the conviction of an innocent man."

As Nelson spoke, Judy Jacobs sat behind her son, her arms crossed her chest, nodding, glancing at the jury. Nodding. Kenny sat further back, his eyes lowered. Withdrawn.

Nelson questioned Kenny's account of where he had been the night of July 4, Kenny's claim that he did not know that Randy watched pornographic videos or that there was money in the house.

He accused the sheriff's department of myopically focusing its investigation on Chris and of conducting an inept investigation.

He suggested Helen committed suicide. He called Wayne Weiler a liar.

He said he would offer evidence to show that Chris had been at the Medford fireworks until 9:30 p.m. and that he had arrived home by 11:20.

He promised to poke holes in the expert testimony, concerning both the shell casings and the tires, and he hinted that there would be some surprises.

"Perhaps more importantly, there is something we expect the evidence will not show," he concluded.

"We expect that there will not be one word of testimony, not one whit of evidence, about what Chris Jacobs is supposed to have done to be involved in the Kunz killings.

"Listen for it throughout the trial," he implored. "Listen to hear if any of the prosecution's evidence has anything at all to say—much less *prove beyond a reasonable doubt*—concerning anything that Chris Jacobs is supposed to have done to be involved in the Kunz killings.

"Ladies and gentlemen, the prosecution has linked Chris Jacobs's name with this crime. They have caused him and his family humiliating publicity. They are prosecuting him for this offense with all the resources of investigation and research at their disposal.

"Now, make them do their job.

"Make them prove this man who sits before you—legally as innocent as you or I—guilty beyond any reasonable doubt.

"It's their burden. Not Chris Jacobs's. Make them meet it.

"Justice demands it. And the law requires it. Make them prove their case.

"You will find they cannot do it."

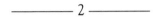

Saturday morning.

Kenny Kunz grasped the rail of the witness stand, swore to tell the truth, and then sat down in a room full of eyes, television cameras, lawyers, microphones, unfamiliar men in suits, young women in dresses, deputies, clocks, shined shoes, reporters, electronic equipment, holsters, ceiling fans, Roddy, carpets, notebooks, Nelson, handcuffs, black-robed judge, Jacobs, pens, remarks one couldn't quite catch, glances, stenographers, codes of behavior, haircuts and also this: emptiness and loneliness, which is all that he brought, packed in his heart, packed in his body, packed in an ill-fitting grey polyester suit.

Kenny told his story, or mostly said "yes" or "no" as Krueger walked him through his family's history, the night of the shootings, the days that followed.

"Kenny, were you at any point in 1987 angry or upset with any of your family members?"

"No."

"Now, you know that they were all killed on or about July 4 of 1987?"

"Yes. They were."

"Did you do it?"

"No."

Lunch. Then it was Nelson's turn.

"Now, Mr. Kunz, didn't you tell Officers Hoenisch and Roddy on July 11, 1987, that one night when you were maybe seven to eight years old, they, that is Helen and Clarence, stopped on the road, a town road to Milan someplace, and they went into the back seat of the old Model A Ford, they used to go there a few times?"

"I don't know."

"You don't recall saying that?"

"I don't recall."

"Excuse me. Do you or do you not recall that you made that response in answer to a question from Officer Roddy asking you, 'Well, would they have sex right in front of you? Where would they have sex?' "

"I don't know. I don't know."

Nelson focused his energies on undermining Kenny's reliability as a witness, pointing out dozens of discrepancies and inconsistencies—some minor, some large—between statements he made to investigators. At the same time, he also kept the jury's attention on the issues of incest, pornography and shame.

"Sir, do you recall telling officers Hoenisch and Roddy that you just liked to read those (pornographic) books. Do you recall saying that?"

"Yes."

"And do you recall telling them on that date that the ones you read are *Penthouse* and *Playboy*?"

"Yes, I had those books."

"Well, is it correct, sir, that you also had other magazines in your trailer—for example, entitled *Meat Eaters*—that might be described as more graphic than *Penthouse* or *Playboy*?"

"Might have been some in there."

Thus having created the impression that Kenny had not been entirely forthcoming about sexual matters:

"Sir, is it correct that you told Officers Hoenisch and Roddy on July 11 of 1987 that Helen and Randy shared a bed?"

"Yes."

"Thank you. Nothing further."

Afterward, Kenny sat a wooden bench outside the courtroom. Germaine sat beside him. For quite a while, neither spoke. Then Germaine gently placed her hand on Kenny's arm.

It was September 7. Marie's birthday. She would have been 75.

On Monday, the jury heard from Dr. Robert W. Huntington, one of the nation's leading pathologists. He was also a bizarre-looking man, a Dr. Seuss cross between a Mennonite and an orangutan.

Concerning Helen, Huntington testified that she died of a single gunshot that entered beneath her jaw, traveled up through the nose and right eye and out the forehead about an inch above the bridge of her nose.

Krueger asked Huntington if he thought the wound had been self-inflicted.

"Highly unlikely. The reason being that when people shoot themselves, generally they tend to come to the midline if they're going to shoot themselves in the head, and they very much tend to shoot back if they're going to shoot themselves in the head, okay?

"So, in other words, yes, from below to above, but, again, had that been suicidal, I would have expected again to the midline and up and back—okay?—so I find it quite, quite unlikely, okay?"

Krueger needed Huntington to be explicit.

"Doctor, do you hold the opinion that you have expressed about the autopsy of Helen Kunz to a reasonable degree of medical certainty?

"With the caveat that you will occasionally see off-angle suicidal shots, yes.

"I still doubt it extremely much. If one were to argue for suicide, I'd want to have the gun right there with her. Absent that and with that particular caveat, yes, sir."

Nelson pressed the suicide issue during his cross examination of Dr. Huntington.

"Would it be correct to say that based solely on your examination of the physical nature of Helen Kunz's wound that you cannot absolutely exclude the possibility of suicide?"

"That's correct, sir. Again, which is the reason for my caveats as stated."

"One of the reasons you said it was unlikely was because there was no weapon found in the vicinity of the remains?"

"Correct, sir."

"And it's usual in your experience for a suicide by firearm that there is also a weapon found in the vicinity of the body?"

"Yes."

"Would I be correct in assuming that it's not usual in your experience for the remains of a suicide victim to be discovered nine months after the fact?"

"It is not usual, no, sir. We have had a few circumstances in which they were discovered very, very late, but again that is the exception rather than the rule."

Nelson then directed the doctor's attention to Randy's autopsy report, reading to him the portion that described "multiple healed and healing purplish-brown scars measuring up to 1.0 centimeters in diameter scattered over the volar aspects of the arms, flanges, entire back, buttocks and upper thighs."

"What," Nelson asked, "is it you are referring to there?"

Huntington looked puzzled.

"Some scars on his skin, sir. But again, notice the lead words, 'multiple healed and healing.' In other words, they appeared to have some real pieces of age on them as by skin growth and color change, okay? Now what those are due to, I don't know."

"Just for my education, what are the volar aspects of the arms?"

"Backs."

"Could those scars that you are referring to there have been needle marks?"

"Not really. No. Because they didn't have the holes in them. You know, you like to see a hole in the middle if you are going to argue for needles, and I really didn't see that. And given the wide distribution, I doubt that, too.

"So, I would say it was much more likely some sort of skin infection—or for heaven's sake—maybe he was dealing with fleas that were just ferocious. But at any event, no. I don't really see the needle marks on them."

"If they were healed scars, could it have been that the needle marks could have healed if they were needle marks?"

"Right. But again, you see, the wide distribution would argue against that. If you are going to inject yourself, you would do it in places other than, for instance, your entire back.

"You know, sort of injecting yourself on your back, it takes talent not given to ordinary people."

Wayne Weiler, who had been Chris's friend since the two were 14, had assisted investigators since the January 1988 round-up, at one point taking deputies for a tour of the swamps and creeks he alleged were used by Chris for dumping stolen car parts.

His enthusiasm for the task of informant fluctuated, and when his moment came to testify that Monday, Krueger found he had caught Weiler at low ebb.

"Wayne," Krueger asked him, "you are testifying here because you have been subpoenaed to testify. Is that right?"

"Right."

"Are you a little nervous about your testimony?"

"Oh, yes."

Still, Wayne was able to get it out that he and Chris had been driving around about a year after he bought the two cars from the Kunzes and that when they passed the Kunzes house "he said there was a roll of money in a drawer."

"Did he say how much or did he do anything to tell you?"

Wayne put his two forefingers together and his two thumbs together and held out his hands.

"He just put his hands like that and said it was a big roll with a rubber band around it."

"Did he describe that roll of money as being all currency?"

"Yes. Hundred dollar bills about."

"Did he say anything else to you about the money?"

"He said he wanted to go back and get it."

Then, to everyone's amazement, a juror spoke up.

"Pardon," she said. "I didn't hear you."

Nelson knew better than to object.

Wayne looked at the juror, then leaned into the microphone.

"He said that he wanted to go back and get it."

Nelson wasted no time in attacking Wayne, but his strikes had to be surgical.

Judge Howard had ruled that unless Chris testified, Krueger would not be allowed to bring Chris's car theft conviction before the jury. That ruling kept Krueger from presenting testimony showing that Chris had hidden stolen car parts in the same general area in which Helen had been discovered. Nelson had to take care that in questioning Wayne, he didn't open a door that would let that testimony in.

"Mr. Weiler, you testified about a conversation that you said you had with Chris Jacobs and that this conversation was in a car when you were driving by the Kunz residence?"

"Yes."

"Was there anyone else in the car with you?"

"No. Just me and Chris."

"As nearly as you can recall, when was that?"

"You want a specific day or year?"

"As specific as you can be."

"There ain't no way I can put a day on that."

"How close can you come."

"About 1984, and that's about as close as I can get."

"Just sometime in 1984?"

"Right."

"You don't remember what month?"

"No."

"You don't remember what time of year?"

"No. I ain't very good at memory."

Nelson's eyes brightened.

"Excuse me?"

"I ain't very good with memory. I am sorry."

Then, quite loudly, Nelson said: "What did you say? You are not very good with your memory?"

Wayne looked confused.

"Right," he said. "With dates."

On the sixth day of testimony—Thursday, October 12—Special Prosecutor Rand Krueger informed the court that there would be a change in testimony of the prosecution's star witness, Peter McDonald.

McDonald, Krueger said, had been in Wausau all week waiting to testify. McDonald was given a chance to review the FBI's tire identification work by William Bodziak and had come to agree with some of Bodziak's conclusions.

Previously, McDonald had positively identified the left rear Duralon tire on Chris Jacobs' car as matching a tire print found in the Kunzes' garden.

Bodziak had positively identified one of the BF Goodrich tires seized from the Jacobses' yard. The left rear Duralon tire was consistent with the track, Bodziak said, but he couldn't make a positive identification.

Krueger told the court that McDonald, after reviewing photographs of the tire tracks enhanced by the FBI, now agreed with Bodziak that the BF Goodrich tire was a positive match.

Krueger asked Howard to permit expanded questioning of McDonald.

Public Defender John Reid had a fit.

McDonald's expanded testimony was an unfair surprise, and violated rules of evidence, Reid said. The state had been preparing its tire evidence for months upon months, even delaying the start of the trial for several weeks while it reviewed more tire evidence reports. To spring this on the defense midway through the trial was unjust, Reid said.

"Chris Jacobs' life is on the line here," Nelson added. "Now the rules have changed in the middle of the game."

Howard shook his head in frustration, but said he would permit the testimony. He then adjourned the trial until Monday to give the defense a chance to regroup.

On Monday, Nelson moved for a mistrial.

"In the middle of a trial, it is simply not possible to change the defense regarding what the state calls the 'linchpin' of the case," Nelson said.

"Surprise is the nature of the beast," Howard said.

And so McDonald got to testify, spending the day on the stand discussing tread sizes and tire composition and measurement strategies. Jurors listened patiently, and patiently waited for McDonald to reach the bottom line, which he uttered near the end of the day, and which became the next day's headline in papers across the state.

From *The Wausau Daily Herald*
Tuesday, October 17:

'NO OTHER TIRE IN THE WORLD'

Expert's testimony links
Jacobs's car, murder site

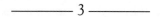

Among his final witnesses, Krueger called Chris's mother, Judy, to the stand. Throughout the trial, she had remained seated behind her son, and as she walked past the defense counsel's table, she touched his shoulder.

She wore a V-neck sweater and gingham shirt. Her curly black hair held twists of grey. You could see Chris in her face. In her forehead. Her mouth. She fixed her blue eyes on Krueger and ever so slightly smiled.

Unknown to the prosecutor, a trap had been laid and it was about to spring.

"I'd like to direct your attention to July 4 of 1987," Krueger said. "Did there come a time in the evening of July 4 when you and other members of your family went to the fireworks in Medford?"

"Yes."

"Do you have some knowledge of what your son was doing or did do at or about the time you left for the fireworks?"

"I believe he was coming into the house from doing chores out in the barn when we were getting ready to leave."

"Was he still at home when you left?"

"Yes."

"Do you recall approximately what time it was that you got home from the fireworks?"

"I'd say about quarter after 10 or so."

"Was your son home at the time?"

"No."

"Is it true, Mrs. Jacobs, that neither you nor your husband saw your son the rest of that evening?"

"No, that's not true."

Alarms went off in Krueger's head. During the John Doe investigation, Mrs. Jacobs had testified under oath that after leaving for the fireworks display, she had not seen her son until the next morning.

"When is the next time you saw him?"

"I saw him at, I would say, about quarter to 12."

Krueger was shocked.

"Quarter to 12 *p.m.*?"

"Quarter to 12 *a.m.*"

"Fifteen minutes before *midnight*?"

"Fifteen minutes before midnight.

"We had a fresh cow that night. I have it on the calendar, and the night that cow freshened, I remember him being home. There was lots of specific things about that freshening that I remember. And when I looked at that calendar and saw that cow freshened that night, I know he was home."

Krueger remained calm and thought fast.

"That's based upon your examination of a calendar that you guys keep, is that right?"

"Right. The cow freshened this year—she's a little Jersey cow— and when she freshened this year, she had a nice little Jersey calf and I told myself, I said, 'Remember the last time she freshened last year? She had that great big black calf.' She was bred to a Holstein bull. And that night he came home early, and that night was on the calendar. July 4."

Krueger confronted her with her John Doe testimony.

"That's what I believed at the time until I saw this calendar. I definitely remember the night Lumpy freshened. She's a little Jersey."

When Krueger pressed Judy about the alibi Chris had given to Roddy and Hoenisch, she was ready.

"You are aware, are you not, that Chris at one point told the police that he was with Annette Harley on the Fourth of July, 1984?"

"He was with Annette Harley day and night from the time they were going together when they just about met so, I assume, he wasn't thinking. He just said, 'I was with Annette' because he was always with Annette."

Judy had one more surprise for Krueger.

"Mrs. Jacobs, I assume that you're acquainted with the fact that your son bought a couple of cars from Kenneth Kunz in 1984. Is that right?"

"Yes."

"Did he also tell you that he was back at the Kunz place in the spring of 1987?"

"No."

Krueger reminded her of her testimony during the John Doe hearing.

"I don't remember much about that testimony at all," she said.

She told Krueger that her testimony during the John Doe hearing was based on a misunderstanding, and that she had gotten it cleared up while preparing for trial.

"Are you saying you did not testify truthfully during the John Doe?" Krueger asked.

"I'm saying that whatever I said at the time, I thought was the truth," she replied.

Then it was Nelson's turn to cross examine.

"Do you know what time Chris got home that night?"

"He got home at 11:20. I have a clock—a digital clock radio—by my bed. And when he drove in, I looked at that. I attempted to go back to sleep, but I have PMS and, at that time, my legs hurt, and I had ached all over and was extremely tired, and that is why I was mad, because he had woke me up. But he did come home early, and I was in the habit of looking at the clock when he come home and said, 'Well, he's safe for tonight. He's home.'

"So, I got up and took some aspirins. About 11:30, I thought that cow is out in the barn and she was pacing. This is summer. Normally, the cows don't stay in the barn in the summer. She was pacing.

"I went out to check her, and I saw she had feet showing already and they looked large, and you could see black coming out on the fur part.

"So, I went back in and I thought, 'Well, Christy just got home. I can ask his help.' I hollered up at him, and he answered. I asked him, I says, 'Will you come pull this calf? It looks like a big one.'

"So he got up, and he came down in his town clothes yet. He did put his barn shoes on."

"What time was that?"

"I would say probably 25 to, quarter to 12."

"What happened then?"

"Well, he came with me and we did pull the calf, and it was a big calf for a Jersey. I'd say 80 pounds, 85 pounds. That's big. A Jersey's only half the size of a Holstein. After we pulled the calf, then he went back in because he did have clean clothes on, and I attempted to beat the calf and take care—tie it up and stuff. I came in about 1 a.m. and he was back upstairs. I locked the door and went to bed."

"Let me ask one more question, if I may," Nelson said.

"Would you lie for your son?"

"No," she said. She looked toward the jury.

"I have three other little boys at home," she said. "As much as I love him, no."

The defense had succeeded in co-opting what might otherwise had been a dramatic close to the state's case.

But rather than hear Chris Jacobs's mother tearfully admit that she did not know where her son was the night the Kunz family was slain, the jury instead was presented with a picture of Chris Jacobs helping his mom deliver Lumpy's calf.

With that coup, Nelson and Reid began to present their case. It would have two objectives.

The first would be to prove that Chris had been to the Medford fireworks until about 10:30 p.m., thus making it impossible for him to have killed the Kunzes and get home in time to assist Lumpy.

The second would be to give the jury plausible suspects other than Chris. They would not, of course, have to prove that someone besides Chris killed the Kunzes; rather, they would need only to raise enough suspicion to generate reasonable doubt.

To that end, the defense called Tracy Bartlett, a pinched-face, beady-eyed convict with a thin mustache who testified that he bought one ounce of cocaine for $1,800 from Randy and Kenny Kunz three days before the family was slain.

Bartlett claimed he had purchased drugs from the Kunzes four times since 1986, and that Kenny had gotten angry at Randy during the July 1, 1987, sale.

"First he started mumbling and grumbling, then he called Randy some harsh names. He became very loud and irate," Bartlett testified, rocking back and forth, his arms crossed his black shirt.

"He thought Randy was getting the least amount of money he could get for it."

From a Marathon County Sheriff's Department report filed by Detective Roddy:

On August 10, 1988, Detective Hoenisch and I interviewed Tracy L. Bartlett.

Tracy said he was still on probation for worthless checks. He said he was placed on probation in 1985 for worthless checks, but probation was continued because he had not paid the fines and restitution. Tracy said he is also accused of opening a checking account under the name Timothy O'Brien. He said there were approximately seven checks cashed for a total of $1,300.

Tracy said he knew who Randy Kunz was from about 1985 or 1986. He said Randy Kunz was a cocaine user and dealer.

Tracy said that he and his wife took their oldest child to the Fourth of July fireworks at Marathon Park. . . . (H)e heard (Tracy then gave the detectives a name) tell Randy, "You're nothing to me. I'll kill you."

We asked Tracy what he expects in return if this information does prove to be of any value. Tracy advised us that he would be given more time to pay off his fine and restitution.

From a Marathon County Sheriff's Department report filed by Detective Roddy:

On September 5, 1988, Detective Hoenisch and I again interviewed Tracy Bartlett at the Marathon County Jail. Tracy said that after he talked to us last time, he tried to remember more about that July 4.

He remembers that it was not Randy Kunz that he saw at Marathon Park that night with the others. He said it was Wayne Weiler.

Tracy said the group he and his wife saw over the July 4 celebration were (Tracy then gave the detectives a list of names, including Chris Jacobs and Wayne Weiler).

He advised that Jacobs made a statement, "Kunz got a lot of bucks. All those old people got a lot of bucks."

He also said (Tracy gave a name) said, "Yeah. You can just rob and kill them."

He said Wayne Weiler said, "Yeah. Execution style."

When Krueger confronted Bartlett with these investigative reports on cross-examination, Bartlett said the information he had given the detectives was "half-truths and lies."

"The reason I'm telling the truth now is I had help withdrawing from cocaine—and I can think clearly, and I have a responsibility."

The following spring, Tracy Bartlett would plead no contest to one count of perjury stemming from his testimony during Chris Jacob's trial.

"When I was up there, I thought it was all true," he would tell a judge in the perjury case. "I was mistaken."

He would be given a five-year suspended prison sentence, three years probation, and ordered to serve six months in jail.

Nelson continued to keep the jury's attention focused on the Kunzes. He would call 43 witnesses in all. At times, their testimony bordered on the absurd.

Fred Stoltenberg, for example, testified that he delivered sausages to the Kunz home. During one visit, he notices a strange smell and saw what he claimed was a dead cat lying in a pot on the wood stove.

"Helen said, 'Don't worry about it. It's the family cat. He's sleeping.'"

Throughout the trial, Judge Howard showed himself to be a no-nonsense jurist, more inclined to employ a frown than a sharp word to signal his displeasure with an attorney's antics. Not eager, of course, to give Jacobs's defense, should it lose, grounds for an appeal, he kept Krueger on a short rein, but gave the defense more latitude.

Still, Howard had his limits.

He would not permit Nelson to call a man who had dropped off a slightly drunken hitchhiker near Athens July 4.

And, following a 2½-hour hearing outside the presence of the jury, he refused to allow Nelson to present evidence surrounding the 1985 murder of a Taylor County couple. The district attorney in charge of that case testified that there was no connection between the two sets of homicides.

On the final day of the defense's case, Nelson called four witnesses who testified that they saw Jacobs at the Medford fireworks.

On cross, one admitted that he had told investigators that he wasn't sure what night he had seen Jacobs. Two others revealed that they were among family and friends of Chris who pledged land or donated money to help Jacobs meet his $154,600 bail. The fourth described himself as a boyhood friend of the defendant.

That the prosecutor was able to point out connections between these witnesses and Chris is hardly surprising; it is only logical that in order to remember seeing Chris at the fireworks, one would at least have to have known him. And it is unlikely anyone but a friend would have come forward to testify at his trial.

The defense rested without calling Chris. The law does not require the accused to stand up and defend himself. Juries are told as much. Still, human nature expects it.

But Nelson could never call Chris to the stand.

Not without giving Krueger the opportunity to tell the jury that the swamps and creeks a few miles north of the Jacobs farm were not only the repository of Helen Kunz's remains, but also Chris's dumping ground for stolen car parts.

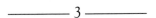

——— 3 ———

Closing arguments began Friday morning, Oct. 27.

Chris Jacobs, Jr., who had not attended any of the trial, came with Judy, arriving well before the arguments started. He was strikingly awkward as he entered the courtroom, walking with the shuffled, uncomfortable gait of a backslider returning to church.

Judy led Chris Jr. to her usual spot, on the bench just behind Chris III, but found that it was already occupied by Kenny and Germaine. She and Chris Jr. sat down directly behind them.

Krueger's closing was as technical and as detailed as his opening, and it lasted close to three hours. It was punctuated with flashes of emotion, but Krueger knew that if he was to win his case, the jurors would have to use their heads. They would have to look at the science, understand it at least well enough to have confidence in it, and use it to draw logical conclusions.

So he went through it all again: the tracks, the bullets, which expert said what, how they compared, how they supported each other.

But, Krueger said, "this case is not about drugs, not about tires, not about shell casings.

"It's about people—these people and anyone else who was at the Kunz place, where they should not have been, for purposes so evil as anyone could conjure up."

He called the defense "a smoke screen," and said, "If this were a football game, the second half should have been canceled."

And he defended Kenny.

"Do you honestly think that he would have conjured up such an elaborate scenario?" Krueger asked, echoing the judge who presided over Helen Kunz's rape trial.

"Then kill his own mother, deny her a Christian burial, and leave her body in the woods to be picked at by animals?"

"Assuming all this, how does he get his hands on the defendant's car so he can put the defendant's tire tracks in the garden?

"Even if you give the defendant the benefit of the doubt, there's a hole in it big enough to drive a murder through."

The hole, countered Nelson, was in the state's case.

"The defense doesn't have to prove anything," he argued.

"You do not have to find Kenneth Kunz guilty in order to find Chris Jacobs not guilty. You do not have to find Helen Kunz guilty in order to find Chris Jacobs not guilty. You do not have to find Wayne Weiler guilty in order to find Chris Jacobs not guilty.

"You only have to have a reasonable doubt in your mind. And don't some or all of these circumstances cause you to have such a reasonable doubt?"

Nelson then reviewed some of the inconsistencies in Kenny's account to investigators.

"In light of all this, and in light of all the different versions, contradictions of Kenneth's story, isn't it the necessary and obvious conclusion that Kenneth's whereabouts and activities on the night of

July 4 and in the early hours of July 5 simply cannot be substantiated from the time he left Wally and Bernie's Bar with his 24-pack of cans and arrived at the Apfelbecks' the next morning?"

He then focused on Helen, quoting Roddy as saying, "It is so highly coincidental that Helen would buy bullets and make a statement that she should kill them all, and then three weeks later everybody is found dead."

"Why would she buy bullets if she didn't have a gun, right?" Nelson asked.

"What are the odds that a stranger or a virtual stranger would pick that time to go to the house to rob or try to rob, and end up killing the family?

"What are the odds that this family should be—as is apparent from the evidence—addicted to pornography, with incest occurring—or at least the belief on Kenneth's part that it may be occurring?

"And that is the important part. What's his state of mind? What does he believe? Not what does a birth certificate show, but what does he believe?

"What are the odds that that would be going on in that family and would play absolutely no part in what happened?

"What are the odds that Kenneth Kunz should leave home and say he spent a holiday night at his place of work drinking beer—even though he knew he wasn't supposed to, even though he was very fearful of losing his job if he had alcohol on company property, even though he wasn't scheduled to work the next day and didn't have to spend the night there in order to be on time for work?

"What are the odds that a stranger or a virtual stranger would pick that night to go there and rob and kill the Kunz family?

"As Officer Roddy pointed out, it is just so highly coincidental."

The jury began deliberations about 5 p.m. Later, a juror would say that the panel had agreed on its verdict almost immediately, but decided to go through the evidence just to make sure. At 10:30, they announced they were through for the night.

At 1 p.m. the next day, they read their verdict to the court.

They had found Chris Jacobs III not guilty on all five counts.

AFTERWORD

From a letter by Germaine Pecher:

Mr Crocker Stephenson. I wonder why you have to print all the worst you can see in my family. they were a good family. didn't hurt any one always minded their own bussiness they didn't have indoor plumbing & maybe had some pornographic Videos but that doesnt make them bad people I can name you several people that don't have indoor plumbing. how can you write a book to make money on some one else's sorrow don't you have any sense of feeling for people I am still suffering the loss of my family. What are you going to write about, no one has been convicted of the crime. just because my family weren't outgoing. is that what you want to write about.

INDEX